Alfred's Teach Your Child To Play Ukulele

Book 1

Ages 5 and Up

The Easiest Ukulele Method Ever!

Nathaniel Gunod
L. C. Harnsberger
Ron Manus

Alfred Music
P.O. Box 10003
Van Nuys, CA 91410-0003
alfred.com

ISBN-10: 1-4706-1883-4 (Book & CD)
ISBN-13: 978-1-4706-1883-4 (Book & CD)

Cover and interior illustrations by Jeff Shelly.

Alfred Cares. Contents printed on environmentally responsible paper.

To the Parents

Ukulele has become one of the most popular instruments in the world. It is featured in popular music and is played in a variety of folk styles. Its portability makes it great for accompanying solo or group singing, so having a ukulelist in the family can add a fun element to family gatherings of all kinds. Consequently, many parents want to share the joy of music-making on the ukulele with their children. They begin this process by teaching children the basics of ukulele before getting them involved in formal lessons with a professional teacher.

About This Book

This book is designed for any family wishing to get their young children started on the ukulele, including those involved in homeschooling who wish to add it to the curriculum. It makes no assumptions of knowledge or skill on the part of the parent. Anyone, whether they have ever played music before or not, can use this book with their child. The step-by-step method provides lessons in the basics of music, while enabling students to start strumming chords to play along with fun children's songs right away. The accompanying audio demonstrates how the music sounds, and each lesson is explained in clear, plain language that is easy to understand.

A Parent Guide page precedes each student page. Most guide pages suggest steps for introducing the page to the student, follow-up practice ideas, and suggestions for reviewing the concepts and/or skills in subsequent lessons. To help with planning, space is often provided where parents can write notes pertaining to the lessons.

The CD contains a recording of every example in the book. It is fun for the student to listen or play along, but more importantly, it will reinforce musical concepts such as rhythm and dynamics. For convenience, you may download the audio onto an MP3 player or other digital music player, such as an iPod.

About the Lessons

Parents should set aside a regular lesson time each week for the child and strictly adhere to this schedule. It can be made a fun, pretend time for you both, where the student must knock to enter the lesson room and call the parent "Teacher." This will help make lesson time a special time, separate from normal family activities. Any parent can be very effective getting a child started on the ukulele, but at some point the child will need the guidance of a professional ukulelist/teacher. Another teacher should be sought when the materials are beyond the parent's understanding, or when lessons create tension in the household.

Page 96 contains some frequently asked questions about teaching a child. Enjoy sharing music and the ukulele together!

Contents

Selecting Your Ukulele

The ukulele you choose for your child can make a significant impact on their success in learning to play. Make sure your child's instrument can be tuned properly and that all the strings ring clearly when plucked, without any additional, unmusical sounds.

Intonation

Intonation refers to the accuracy of the pitch, or, put another way, whether or not a voice or instrument is *in tune*. Intonation problems are common among inexpensive ukuleles. In other words, they can be tuned to sound good on the first few frets, but not on every part of the instrument. This can cause frustration later on, so be sure to ask the music store's fretted-instrument specialist about the intonation of the ukuleles you are considering.

The Action

Some ukuleles are more difficult to play because the strings are set too high off the fretboard and are thus difficult to press down. The distance (gap) between the strings and the frets of the ukulele is called the *action*. It is possible, of course, for the action to be set too low, causing unpleasant rattling noises on every note or strum. Either of these conditions—an action that is high or too low—would cause frustration for the student. When shopping for your ukulele, be sure to ask the music store's fretted-instrument specialist about the action of the ukuleles you are considering. See if you can have your child try the Butterfly Finger Exercise on page 16. If it is too difficult for the child to press down the string, the action may be set too high.

Selecting Your Ukulele

Ukuleles come in different types and sizes. There are four basic sizes: *soprano*, *concert*, *tenor*, and *baritone*. The smallest is the soprano, and they get gradually bigger, with the baritone being the largest.

Soprano, concert, and tenor ukes are all tuned to the same notes, but the baritone is tuned to different notes. Each uke has a different sound. The soprano has a light, soft sound, which is what you expect when you hear a ukulele. The larger the instrument, the deeper the sound. Some tenor ukuleles have six or even eight strings.

The soprano ukulele is the most common, but you can use soprano, concert, and four-string tenor ukuleles with this book. Because the baritone uke is tuned to the same notes as the top four strings of the guitar, you can use *Alfred's Kid's Guitar Method Book 1* to start learning on that type of ukulele.

Parts of the Ukulele

Most young children will be happy with whatever type of ukulele a parent provides. Sometimes, though, a child is motivated to learn ukulele through their admiration of style or color of an instrument. When possible, it is a good idea to allow the student to use the ukulele of their choice, so they will be motivated to pick it up and practice playing every day.

Introducing the Parts of the Ukulele

For a very young child, it can be fun to make up a name for the ukulele, and introduce it to your child as a new friend with three main parts—a head, neck, and body—just like a person!

1. While you carefully hold your child's ukulele, oriented vertically, with the bottom of the instrument lightly resting on your lap and the headstock in one hand, introduce the headstock, neck, and body by pointing with the other hand while you say the name.

2. Now, play a game where you point to the part and your child says its name. Make the pointing-and-naming game fun! Perhaps choose some appropriate prizes for correct answers.

Practice Suggestions

1. At every lesson or practice session, introduce one or two new parts.

2. Play the pointing-and-naming game including all the parts that have been covered in your sessions.

3. Be sure to impress upon your child the importance of being gentle with their new friend!

Subsequent Lessons

Continue to add new parts to the game at every session until your child knows the names of the parts so well, the game loses its luster. It's a good idea, however, to bring the game back every once in a while, just to make sure your child remembers the parts. It can be a good way to break up a serious lesson and make it more fun.

Parts of the Ukulele

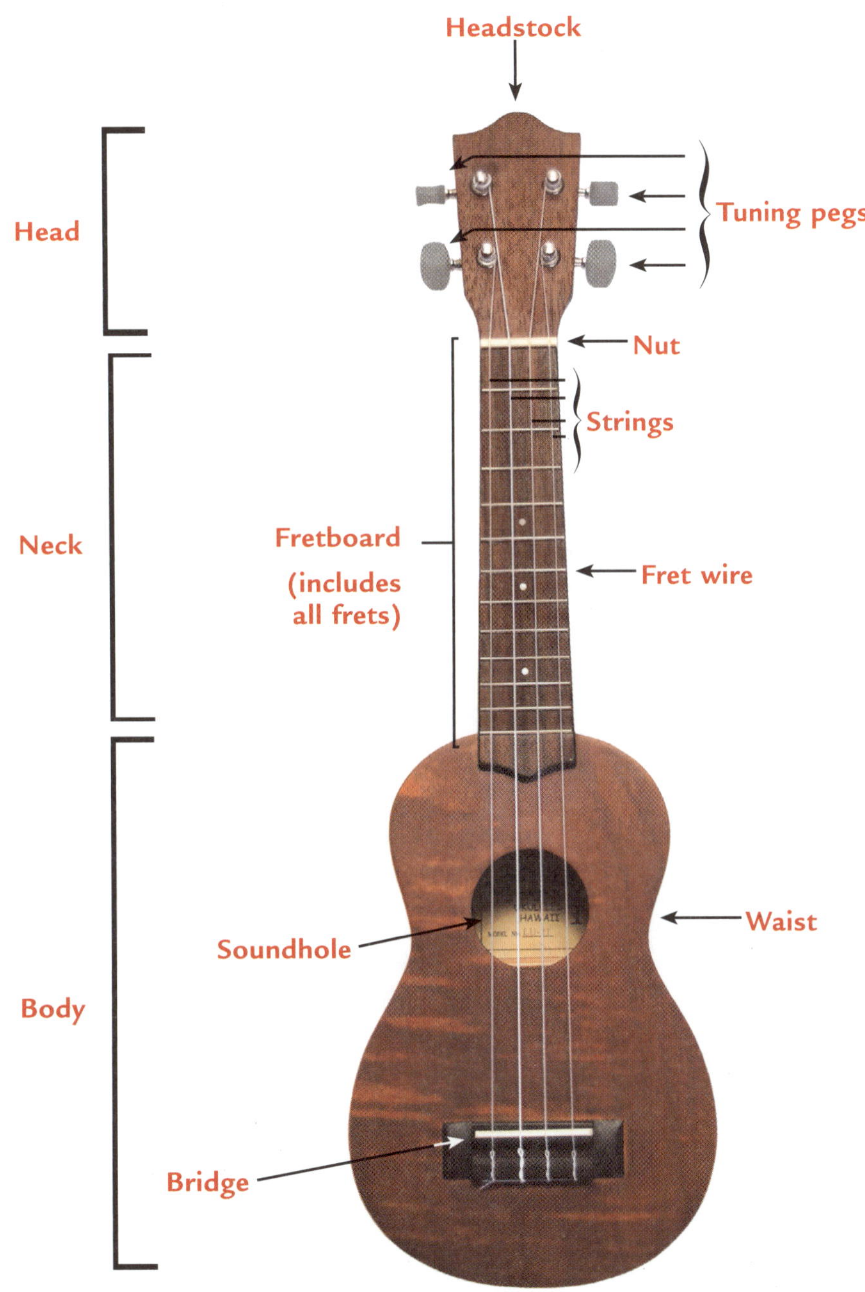

Caring for Your Ukulele

Get to know your ukulele and treat it like a friend. When you carry it, think of it as part of your body so you don't accidentally bump it against walls or furniture, and be especially sure not to drop it! Every time you are done playing, carefully dust off your ukulele with a soft cloth, and be sure to put it away in its case. If you don't have a case, always put it in a safe place where it won't be in the way.

Tuning Your Ukulele

Your child's music-making will be most successful when the ukulele is in tune. While it is possible for a ukulele to be just "in tune with itself," it is best to be in tune with a standard pitch from either an in-tune piano, a tuning fork, a pitch pipe, or the audio recording that comes with this book. You can also use an electronic tuner or a tuning app for your mobil device that "listens" to each string and tells you whether or not it is in tune. With the ukulele tuned properly, your family sing-alongs can include the ukulele along with other properly tuned instruments.

Stringing the Ukulele

Strings do not last forever. A professional ukulelist changes strings fairly often, so their ukulele always sounds its best. Old strings can sound dull and lifeless, and eventually become difficult to tune. Until your child is old enough to string the instrument, it will be up to you to make sure it is strung correctly before getting it in tune. Take the instrument to a local music store and have someone lead you step-by-step through the process of changing the strings. Alternatively, ask them to do it for you!

There are different styles of headstocks and tuning pegs, but your ukulele will be strung when you buy it, so observe how it is done and even take a photograph. That way, when it is time to replace a broken string (it happens), or put on a whole new set, you'll have a model to follow. Strings should go from the inside to the outside, so that turning the peg counterclockwise tightens it, making it sound higher. Turning the peg clockwise should loosen the string, making it sound lower.

On a ukulele, the string closest to the floor when the ukulele is held normally (with the left hand holding the notes on the neck and the right hand strumming and/or plucking the strings) is the first string.

Getting in Tune

Following the directions on page 9 will get your ukulele in tune, but they all require careful listening. One learns to be very discriminating about intonation with experience. An electronic tuner is a good tool for learning good intonation, as it will show you whether a string is *sharp* (too high) or *flat* (too low), and by how much.

Be very careful when tuning a string up or tightening it. Tuning a string too high can cause it to break. Always listen as you slowly turn the peg, bit-by-bit. That way, you'll hear if you are turning the peg too rapidly and tuning the string too high. In other words: never turn a tuning peg without plucking the string and listening.

Tuning Your Ukulele

First make sure your strings are wound properly around the tuning pegs. They should go from the inside to the outside, as in the picture to the right.

Turning a tuning peg clockwise makes the pitch lower. Turning a tuning peg counterclockwise makes the pitch higher. Be sure not to tune the strings too high because they could break!

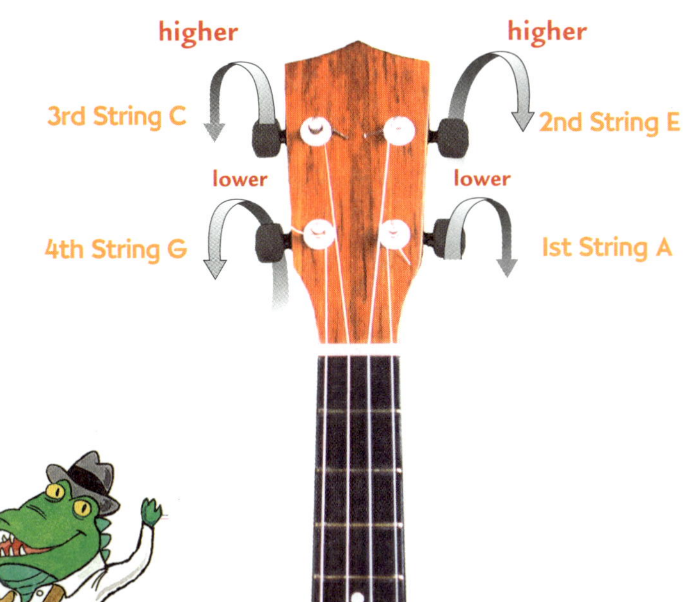

Important:

Always remember that the string closest to the floor is the first string. The one closest to the ceiling is the fourth string.

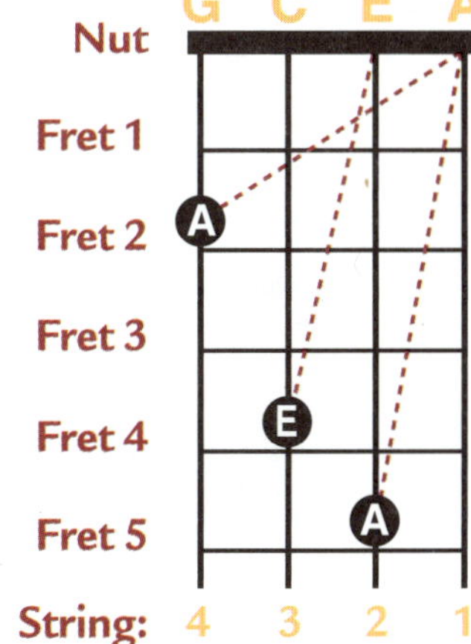

Tuning with the CD or DVD

Tracks 1 & 2

Using Your CD

Put the CD in your CD player and play Tracks 1 and 2. Listen to the directions and match each of your ukulele's strings to its pitch on the CD.

Using Your DVD

Put the DVD in your computer or DVD player. Go to the Scenes menu and click on Tuning. Follow the directions and listen carefully to get your ukulele in tune.

Tuning without the CD or DVD

Tuning the Ukulele to Itself

When your first string is in tune, you can tune the rest of the strings just using the ukulele alone. First tune the first string to A on the piano, then follow the instructions to the right to get the ukulele in tune.

Press fret 5 of string 2 and tune it to the pitch of string 1 (A).

Press fret 4 of string 3 and tune it to the pitch of string 2 (E).

Press fret 2 of string 4 and tune it to the pitch of string 1 (A).

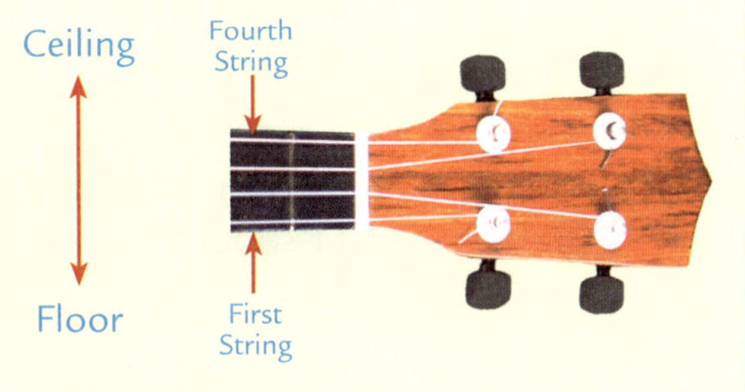

Pitch Pipes and Electronic Tuners

If you don't have a piano available, buying an electronic tuner or pitch pipe is recommended. The salesperson at your music store can show you how to use them.

How to Hold Your Ukulele

The position of the student's body and the position of the ukulele relative to the student's body are the foundations of their ukulele technique. With the body and hands positioned optimally, learning the ukulele is easiest. Your child should always have good posture when playing the ukulele and be aware of the ukulele's position.

Introducing the Concept

While there is not one correct way for your child to hold the ukulele (page 11 shows just a few of the available options), there are some common-sense guidelines to keep in mind for the best results:

1. The student's spine should be straight. Avoid leaning to the right or left, or "hunching over" the instrument.

2. The shoulders should be level. Avoid elevating either shoulder, or thrusting it forward or backward.

3. The left hand should be able to comfortably reach every fret, from the lowest to the highest, without changing the position of the spine or either shoulder.

4. The right arm should be able to move freely from the elbow, up and down, without feeling limited by the outer edge of the ukulele body or moving the right shoulder.

Practice Suggestions

1. Check the four points above every time your child gets ready to play.

2. Recheck their posture before each example or song.

Subsequent Lessons

Don't worry if you have to work on posture and position at every lesson. This will be an ongoing process and will require attention for quite some time.

Notes:

How to Hold Your Ukulele

Hold your ukulele in the position that is most comfortable for you. Some positions are shown below.

Rest the ukulele gently on your thigh.

Cradle the ukulele with your right arm by gently holding it close to your body. Your right hand should be free to strum it.

When you practice on your own or want to play just for fun, you might feel comfortable sitting cross-legged on the floor or on your bed. Just be sure to keep good posture with your back straight.

Strumming the Strings

Now that your child is holding the ukulele properly, it is time to begin playing. Strumming will be a fun and exciting activity. The idea is to brush quickly across all four strings, causing them all to sound together.

Strumming with a Pick

A ukulele *pick*, or *plectrum*, is generally made of one uniform material, such as plastic or nylon. They are usually triangle shaped, with two of the corners very rounded and one slightly less rounded. The less-rounded corner is typically the part used to strike the strings.

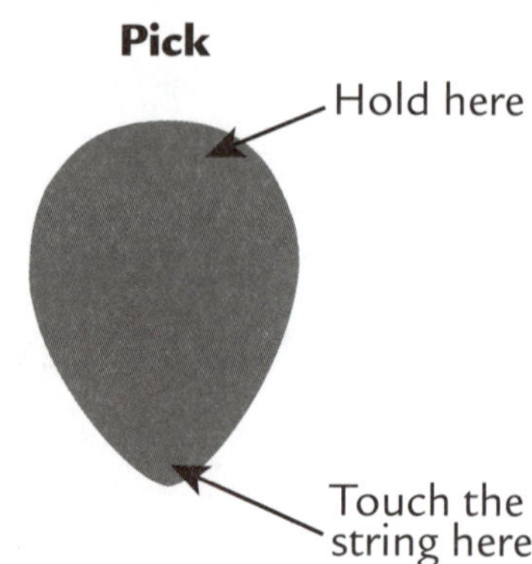

Introducing the Pick

1. Help your child get into a good position with their ukulele, ready to play.
2. Show them the pick and point out the less-rounded corner, explaining that it is the strumming end. Demonstrate strumming with the pick.
3. Have your child hold their right arm out in front of them, keeping the forearm in contact with the body of the ukulele.
4. Have them hold their fingers in a comfortably curled position, like holding a ball.
5. Place the pick on the tip joint of the finger, with the less-rounded corner pointed out, away from the palm of the hand.
6. Have your child place their thumb on the pick and hold it firmly. Make sure they don't squeeze the pick too hard...they should just hold it firmly in place.
7. Help the student place the tip of the pick on the 4th string (the one closest to them, if they're holding the instrument correctly), and, moving from the wrist with a little help from the elbow joint, move it quickly and firmly across all four strings to create a strum.

Strumming with the Fingers

Some students prefer to strum with their fingers. Two popular ways to do this are: 1) with the thumb, or 2) with the back of the nail of the index finger. Either way is fine. Demonstrate both methods and have your child try both. The pictures on page 13 show strumming with the pick and with the fingers.

Practice Suggestions

1. Tap a slow, steady beat on your lap, and count aloud, saying "1 2 3 4 5 6 7 8."
2. Using their chosen strumming method, have them strum the strings while counting aloud.
3. Play along with Track 3 on the CD.

Subsequent Lessons

1. If using a pick, remind the student to hold it firmly but not to squeeze too hard. The idea is to make a solid, firm sound.
2. Always encourage your child to keep a slow, steady beat as they strum.

Strumming the Strings

To *strum* means to play the strings with your right hand by brushing quickly across them. There are two common ways of strumming the strings. One is with a pick, and the second is with the fingers.

Strumming with a Pick

Hold the pick between your thumb and index finger. Hold it firmly, but don't squeeze it too hard.

Strum from the fourth string (closest to the ceiling) to the first string (closest to the floor).

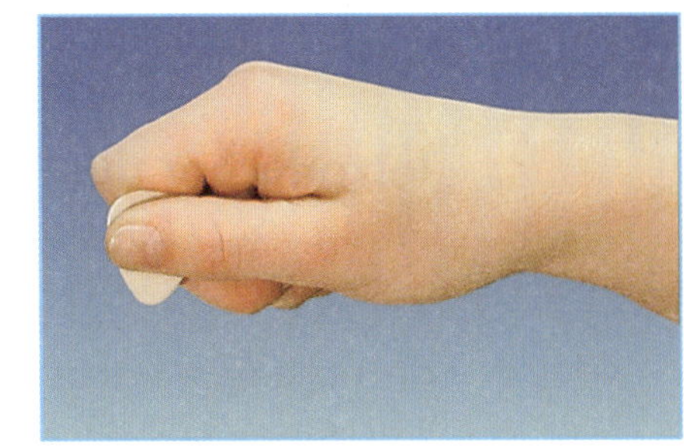

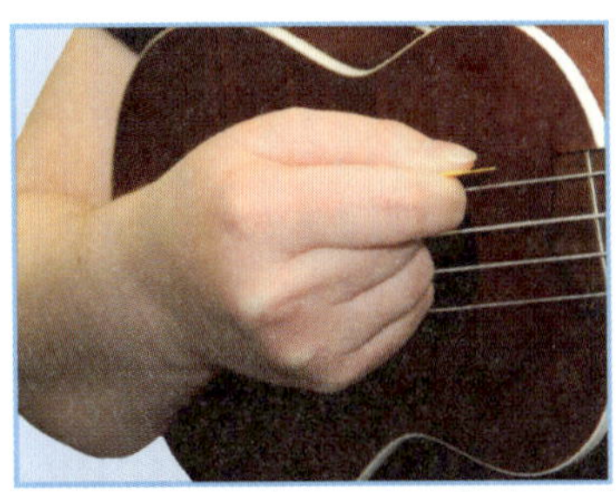

Start near the top string.

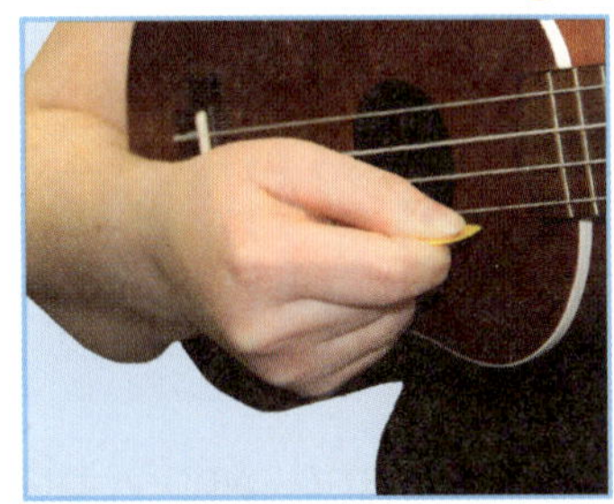

Move mostly your wrist, not just your arm. Finish near the bottom string.

Strumming with Your Fingers

First decide if you feel more comfortable strumming with the side of your thumb or the nail of your index finger. The strumming motion is the same with the thumb or finger as it is when using the pick. Strum from the fourth string (closest to the ceiling) to the first string (closest to the floor).

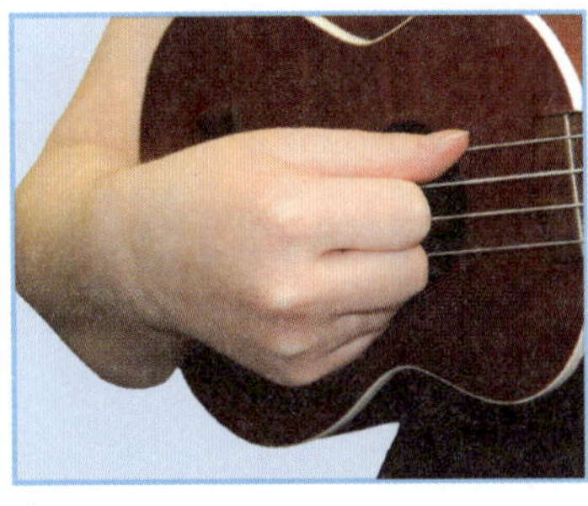

Strumming with the thumb

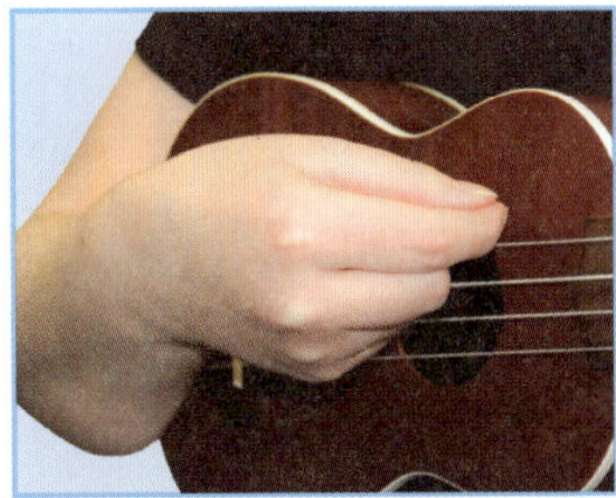

Strumming with the index finger

Important:

Strum by mostly moving your wrist, not just your arm. Use as little motion as possible. Start as close to the top string as you can, and never let your hand move past the edge of the ukulele.

Time to Strum!  Track 3

Strum all four strings slowly and evenly.
Count your strums out loud as you play.
Repeat this exercise until you feel comfortable strumming the strings.

	strum	strum	strum	strum	strum	strum	strum	strum
	/	/	/	/	/	/	/	/
Count:	1	2	3	4	5	6	7	8

Strumming Notation

Ukulele strums are often written with slash-style notation. Most notational styles indicate how long each musical sound lasts. We measure musical time with *beats*, which are the steady pulse of the music. The *rhythm* is the pattern of note durations against the beat. A *quarter-note* strum is written with a slash and a stem, as shown on page 15. A quarter-note slash gets one beat.

Introducing the Page

Discuss beats with the student. Relating beats to the steady tick-tock of a clock is helpful. Introduce the *staff* as a picture of the time in which the music will happen, and the *bar lines* as a way to divide the time into groups of beats, called *measures*. The *time signature*, which always appears at the beginning, is there to tell us how many beats go in each measure.

Practice Suggestions

1. Point to the quarter-note slashes in "More Time to Strum" and count aloud, slowly and evenly, saying "1 2 3 4 1 2 3 4."

2. Strum across the strings while counting aloud. Do this several times, until it is easy.

3. Now, counting aloud slowly and evenly, play "More Time to Strum" on just the top three strings.

Subsequent Lessons

1. Make it part of the routine to point at the notes of a song or example while slowly and evenly counting aloud.

2. Play along with Track 4 of the CD.

Notes:

Strumming Notation

Beats

Each strum you play is equal to one *beat*.
Beats are even, like the ticking of a clock.

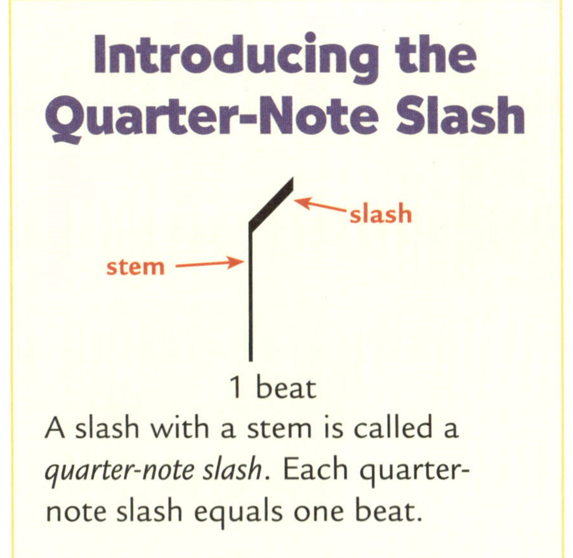

Introducing the Quarter-Note Slash

A slash with a stem is called a *quarter-note slash*. Each quarter-note slash equals one beat.

The Staff and Treble Clef

Ukulele music is usually written on a five-line *staff* that has a *treble clef* at its beginning.

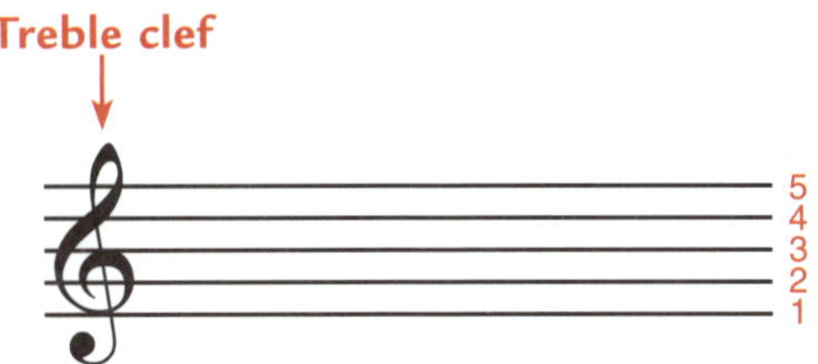

Bar Lines, Measures, and Time Signatures

Bar lines divide the staff into equal parts called measures. A *double bar line* is used at the end to show you the music is finished.

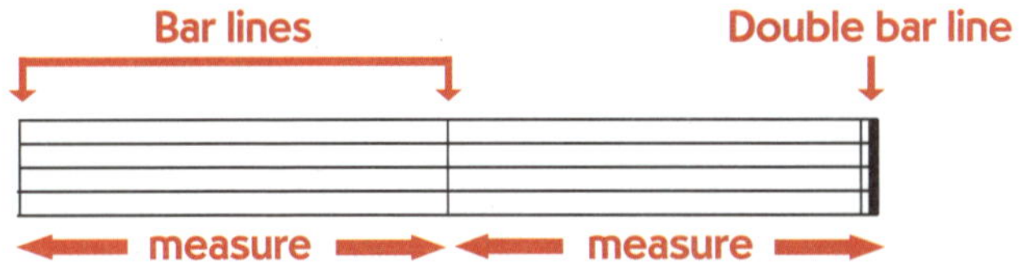

Measures are always filled with a certain number of beats. You know how many beats are in each measure by looking at the time signature, which is always at the beginning of the music. A $\frac{4}{4}$ time signature ("four-four time") means there are 4 equal beats in every measure.

More Time to Strum

Track 4

Play this example in $\frac{4}{4}$ time. It will sound the same as "Time to Strum," which you played on the previous page. Keep the beats even and count out loud.

Strum all four strings as you did before.

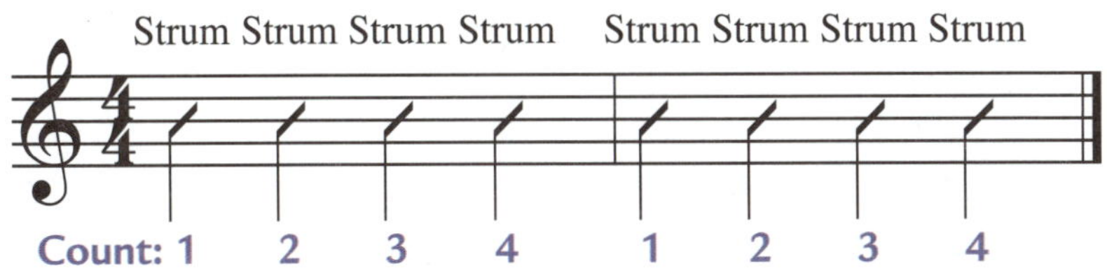

Strumming all four strings

Using Your Left Hand

The job of a left-hand finger is to shorten the vibrating string length by pressing the string into a fret. The shorter the vibrating string, the higher the *pitch* (pitch is the highness or lowness of the sound). Note that we *do not press the string into the wood of the fretboard*. It is by pressing the string securely into the fret wire that we change the vibrating length of the string, so the most efficient left-hand technique is one that accomplishes this using as little strength as necessary. Be sure to review How to Read Chord Diagrams with your child.

Introducing the Left-Hand Fingers

Numbers are given to the left-hand fingers for easy identification. The fingers are numbered consecutively, with the index finger being 1 and the pinky, 4.

1. Have your child hold up their left hand. Point to each finger and say the corresponding finger number.

2. Repeat, but this time, ask your child to say the finger number as you point.

Practice Suggestions

1. Have your child trace their left hand on a separate piece of paper. Then, number each finger.

2. Have your child hold up their left hand. As you call out finger numbers, have them wiggle the correct finger.

Hand Position and Placing a Finger on a String

Fingers are naturally stronger and will provide the best leverage in a curled position, like gently holding a ball. The left thumb should be in the middle of the back of the ukulele neck, between fingers 1 and 2. Keeping the elbow loosely in and the fingers curled, use the very tips of the fingers to press the strings, placing them directly next to the fret wire, but not actually ON the fret.

Practice Suggestion—Butterfly Finger Exercise

1. Using the photos on page 17 as a guide, have your child lightly place finger 1 without pressing down on the 2nd string, right next to the 1st fret. You can say the finger should be "like a butterfly landing on the string."

2. Ask him or her to pluck the 2nd string with the pick or right-hand finger. You will hear a clicking, unpitched sound. No note will be heard.

3. Have your child slowly begin to add pressure with the finger as they pluck the string. The instant the string sings out a clear note, the student should stop adding pressure. That is as hard as they need to press to play.

Subsequent Lessons

Your child may experience a little discomfort at first. It takes a while to develop calluses at the tips of the left-hand fingers. Keep practice sessions short to minimize associating discomfort with playing ukulele, and always remind them that their fingers should not press hard or squeeze the neck. Repeat the "butterfly finger" exercise described above often.

Using Your Left Hand

Hand Position

Learning to use your left-hand fingers easily starts with a good hand position. Place your hand so your thumb rests comfortably in the middle of the back of the neck. Position your fingers on the front of the neck as if you are gently squeezing a ball between them and your thumb. Keep your elbow in and your fingers curved.

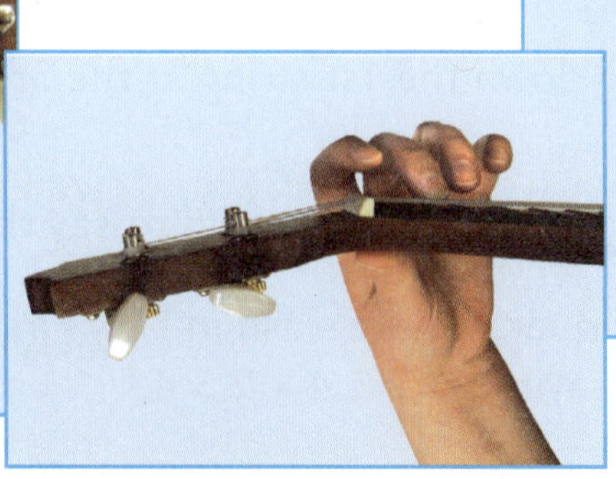

Keep elbow in and fingers curved

Like gently squeezing a ball between your fingertips and thumb

Placing a Finger on a String

When you press a string with a left-hand finger, make sure you press firmly with the tip of your finger and as close to the fret wire as you can without actually being right on it. Short fingernails are important! This will create a clean, bright tone.

RIGHT
Finger presses the string down near the fret without actually being on it.

WRONG
Finger is too far from fret wire; tone is "buzzy" and indefinite.

WRONG
Finger is on top of fret wire; tone is muffled and unclear.

How to Read Chord Diagrams

Chord diagrams show where to place your fingers. The example to the right shows finger 1 on the first string at the first fret. The "o"s above the second, third, and fourth strings tell you these strings are to be played open, meaning without pressing down on them with a left-hand finger.

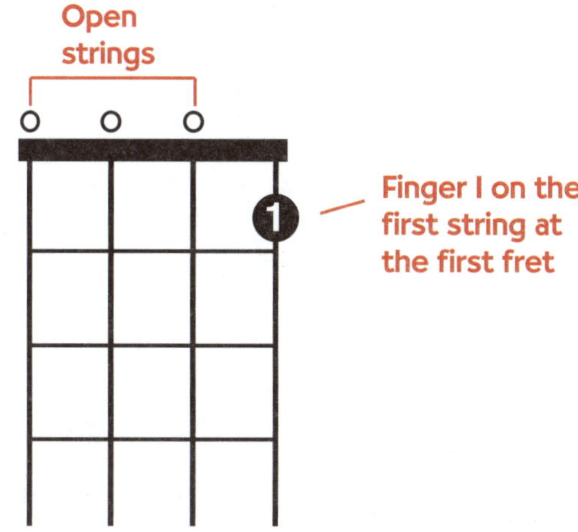

The C Chord

Combined with holding the ukulele properly and a good left-hand position, properly curled fingers will make playing a C chord fun and easy for your child.

Introducing the C Chord

1. Practice strumming the strings using "More Time to Strum" on page 15.

2. Repeat the Butterfly Finger Exercise from page 16.

3. Together, listen to the audio for Track 5.

4. Make sure finger 3 is up on the left side of its very tip, directly to the left of the 3rd fret.

5. While holding down the 1st string at the 3rd fret, strum all four strings.

Practice Suggestions

1. Point at each quarter-note slash in "My First Chord" as you slowly and evenly count aloud, saying "1 2 3 4 1 2 3 4."

2. Counting aloud, slowly strum "My First Chord."

3. When strumming this song feels comfortable and easy, try playing along with the audio for Track 6.

Subsequent Lessons

Continue to remind your child not to squeeze too hard with the 3rd finger. Repeat the Butterfly Finger Exercise on page 16 often. Be patient and allow them to experiment with the finger position, remaining sensitive to potential discomfort. Keep practice sessions short.

Notes:

The C Chord

Use finger 3 to press the 1st string at the 3rd fret. If you have any trouble holding finger 3 down to play the C chord, place fingers 1 and 2 on the 1st and 2nd frets behind finger 3 until you are able to play with just finger 3.

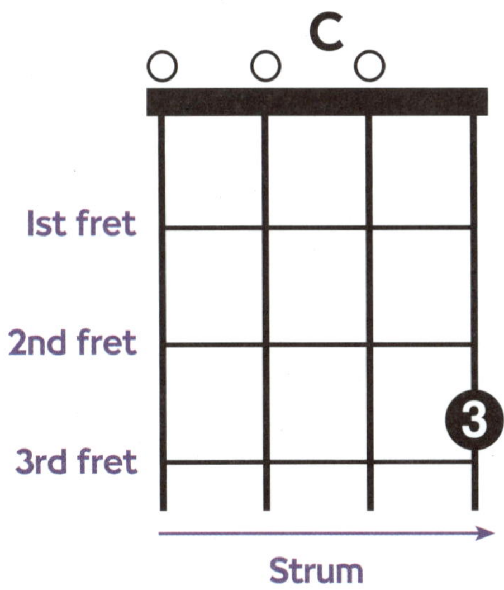

Strumming

Strum the four-string C chord on each quarter-note slash. Make sure your strums are even. Count aloud as you play:

1-2-3-4 | 1-2-3-4.

Listen to the song on the audio to hear how it should sound!

My First Chord

Remember: This means there are 4 beats in each measure.

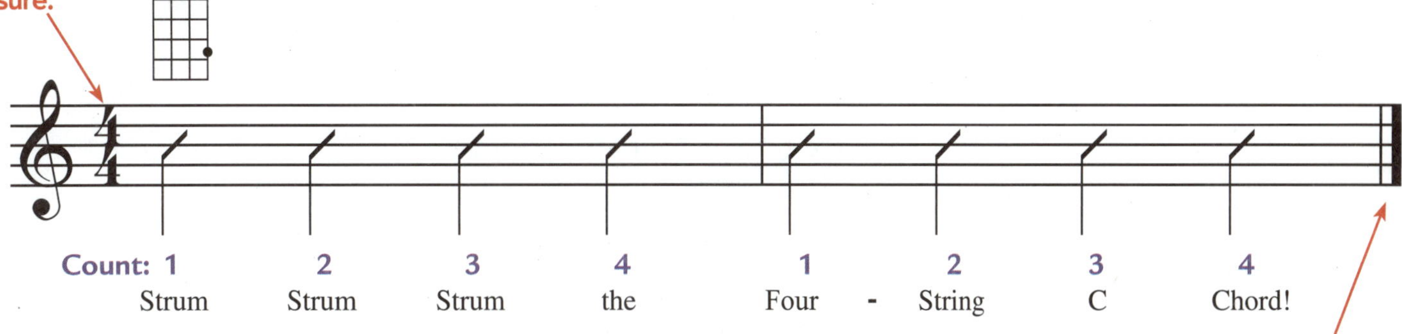

This double bar line tells us the music is finished.

The Quarter Rest

Silence is a very important part of music, and it is indicated with a *rest* symbol. For every note value (such as a quarter note), there is an equal rest duration.

Introducing the Concept

Some say the quarter rest, which means one beat of silence, looks like a bird flying sideways, or a squiggly line. What does it look like to your child? That could be a fun conversation. Discuss the importance of silence in music, and how boring music would be if it never stopped.

1. Try singing "Three Blind Mice" without any silences or pauses. Wouldn't that be silly?

2. Show your child the rest position using the picture on top of page 21 as a reference.

3. Have your child place the pinky-side of their right hand across the strings, just to the left of the bridge. Introduce this as the *rest position*.

4. Now, have your child strum all of four strings, then place their hand in rest position to stop them from ringing.

5. Finally, practice the "Rest Warm-up" while slowly and evenly counting aloud, saying "1 2 3 rest 1 2 3 rest," assuming rest position every time you say "rest."

Practice Suggestions

1. Together with your child, saying "1 2 3 rest 1 2 3 rest," etc., count aloud and point at each note and rest in "Three Blind Mice."

2. Have your child position the left-hand 3rd finger on the C chord, making sure all four strings are ringing clearly.

3. Counting aloud, strum "Three Blind Mice," carefully performing all of the rests using the rest position.

4. Have your child strum through "Three Blind Mice" while you sing the words.

5. Let your child try playing and singing the words themself.

Subsequent Lessons

1. Continue practicing "Three Blind Mice" as needed.

2. Repeat the Butterfly Finger Exercise often.

3. Keep checking to make sure all four strings of the C chord are ringing clearly.

The Quarter Rest

Introducing the Quarter Rest

1 beat

This strange-looking music symbol means to be silent for one beat. Stop the sound of the strings by lightly touching them with the side of your hand, as in the photo.

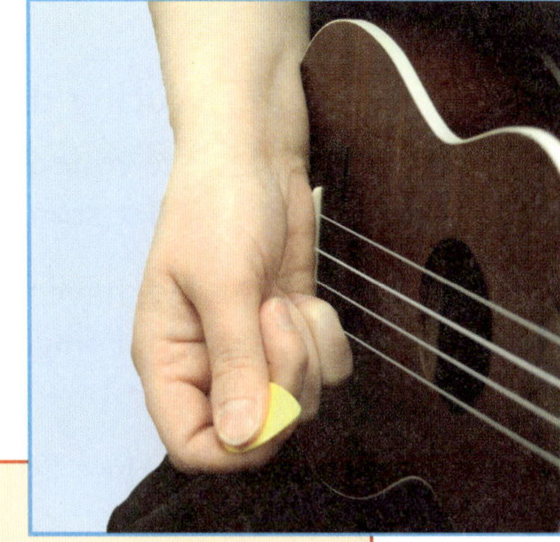

Track 7

Rest Warm-up

Before playing "Three Blind Mice," practice this exercise until you are comfortable playing rests.

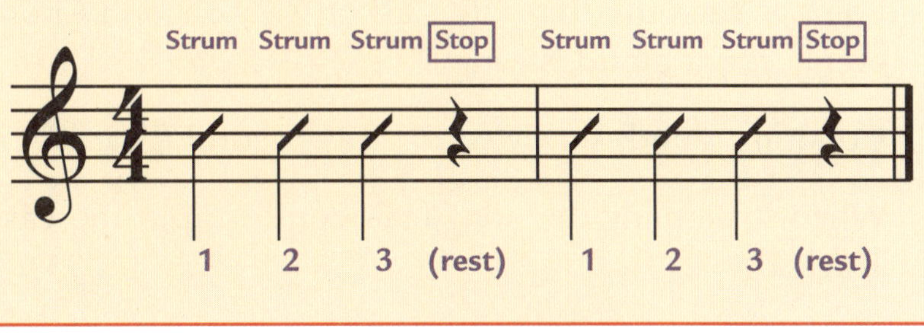

Practice Tip

Strum the chords and have a friend sing the words.

Three Blind Mice

Track 8

C

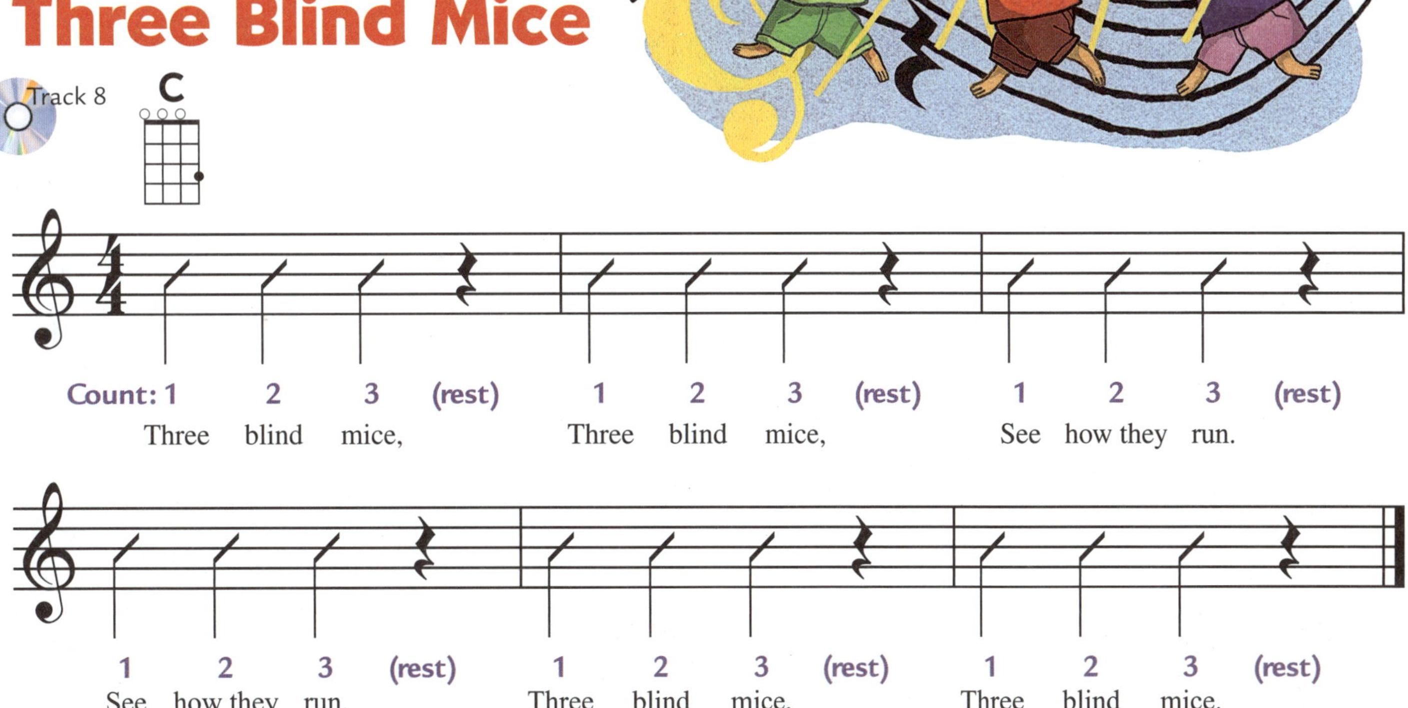

The C⁷ Chord

All "7" chords have a bluesy quality. This one is very easy and is a lot like the C chord. Just use the 1st finger on the 1st string instead of the 3rd.

Introducing the C⁷ Chord

1. Have your child position the left hand for the C chord, with the 3rd finger on the 1st string at the 3rd fret.

2. Now, have them simply remove the 3rd finger from the 1st string, and place the 1st finger at 1st fret. We usually play a little to the left side of the tip of finger 1.

3. Together, listen to the audio for Track 9.

Practice Suggestions

1. Point at each quarter-note slash in "My Second Chord" as you slowly and evenly count aloud, saying "1 2 3 4 1 2 3 4."

2. Counting aloud, slowly strum "My Second Chord."

3. When strumming this song feels comfortable and easy, try playing along with Track 10.

Subsequent Lessons

Continue to remind your child not to squeeze too hard with the 1st finger. Repeat the Butterfly Finger Exercise on page 16 often. Remain sensitive to potential discomfort, and keep practice sessions short.

Notes:

The C⁷ Chord

Track 9

Use finger 1 to press the 1st string at the 1st fret.
This chord is just like the C chord but you are using
your 1st finger and not your 3rd finger.

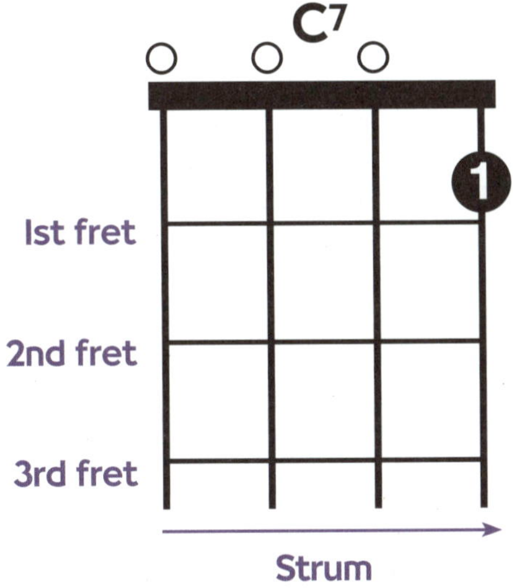

My Second Chord

Track 10

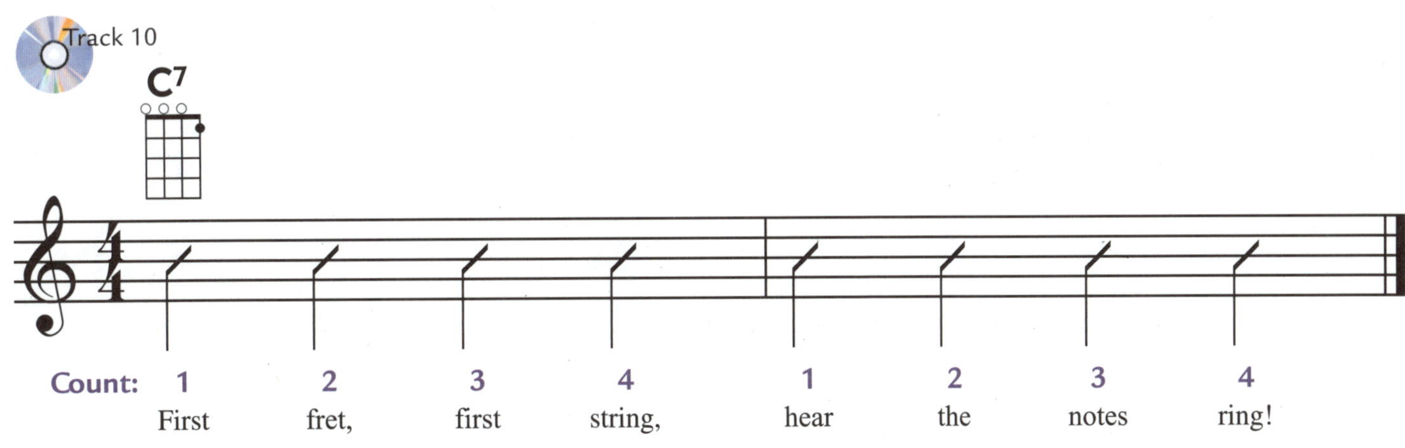

Troubadour Song

This song combines quarter rests with the two chords covered so far. Now is a good time to start singing "Skip to My Lou" around the house. It will be part of your ukulele time, soon!

Introducing the Page

Follow these steps with your child:

1. Point at each note, naming the chord to play or saying "rest" (e.g., "C C C rest C^7 C^7 C^7 rest," etc.).

2. Now, ask your child to do this on their own.

3. Have your child, without strumming, switch the left-hand fingers from C with the 3rd finger to C^7 with the 1st, over and over, until it is easy to do.

Practice Suggestions

1. Play the right hand alone while counting aloud, saying "1 2 3 rest 1 2 3 rest," etc., being careful to use the rest position to perform the quarter rests. You can use the rest as time to move the left hand and switch chords when there is a chord change.

2. Add the left hand, continuing to count aloud.

3. Try playing along with Track 11.

Subsequent Lessons

To your child, remembering to switch chords while performing the rests may feel, at first, a little like patting their head while rubbing their belly—it requires coordination that will have to be practiced. This is one of the many reasons learning an instrument is so wonderful for a young child. Gaining this sort of coordination does a lot for his or her mental development. It is worth the effort!

Notes:

Troubadour Song

Remember to stop the sound by lightly touching the strings with the side of your hand on each ♪. Wait one beat.

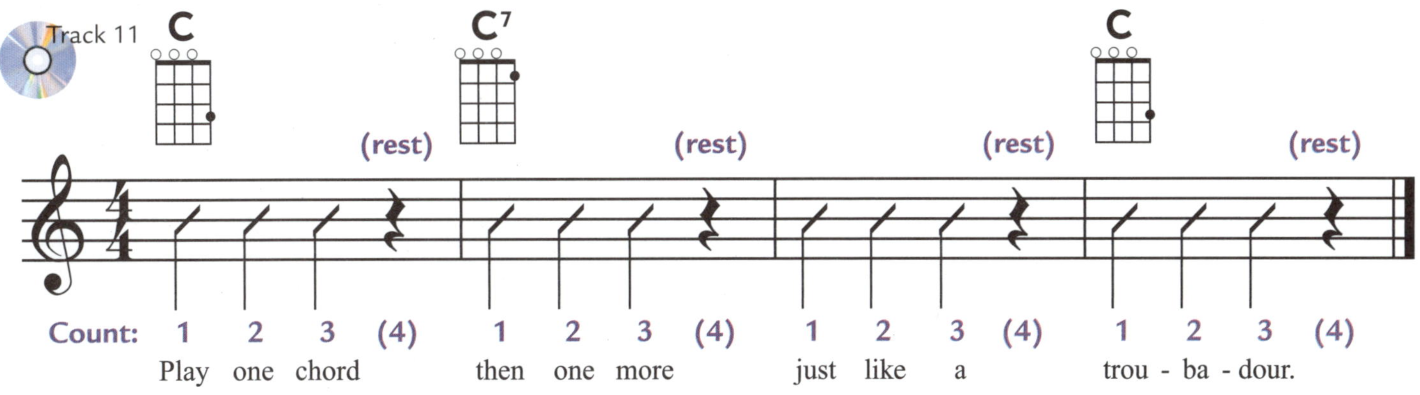

*A troubadour was a musician who traveled around singing and playing.

The F Chord

This is the first chord your child will learn that uses more than one left-hand finger. The F chord uses both the 1st and 2nd fingers.

Introducing the F Chord

1. Have your child position the left hand for the C^7 chord, with the 1st finger on the 1st string at the 1st fret.

2. Now, have them simply remove the 1st finger from the 1st string, and place it on the 2nd string at the 1st fret. We usually play a little to the left side of the tip of finger 1. It's very important to stay up on the tip and avoid bumping into the 1st string, so it can ring clearly.

3. Next, have them add the 2nd finger to the 4th string at the 2nd fret.

4. Together, listen to the audio for Track 12.

Practice Suggestions

1. Point at each quarter-note slash in "My Third Chord" as you slowly and evenly count aloud, saying "1 2 3 4 1 2 3 4."

2. Counting aloud, slowly strum "My Third Chord."

3. When strumming this song feels comfortable and easy, try playing along with Track 13.

Subsequent Lessons

Continue to remind your child not to squeeze too hard with the fingers. Repeat the Butterfly Finger Exercise on page 16 often.

Notes:

The F Chord

This is the first time you are pressing two fingers down at once. First press finger 1 on the 2nd string at the 1st fret. Then use finger 2 to press the 4th string at the 2nd fret. Press both fingers down firmly as you strum all the strings.

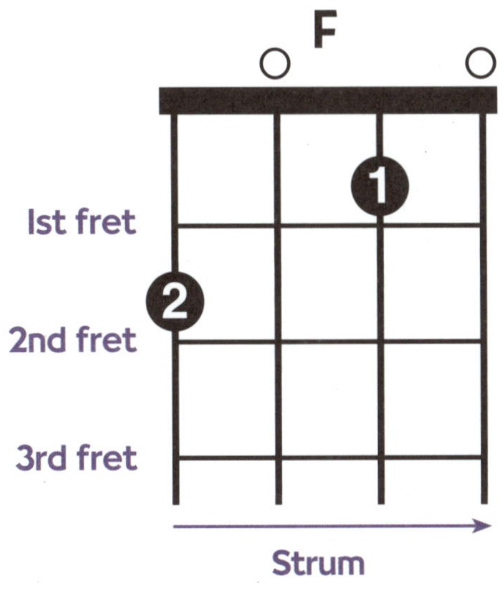

My Third Chord

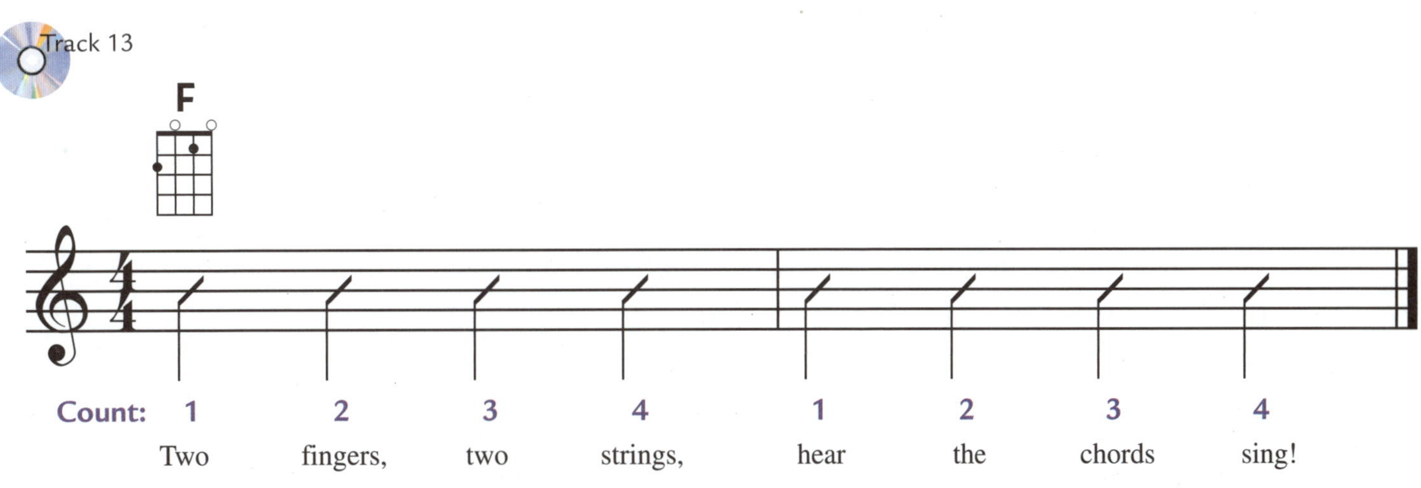

Three Chords in One Song

This song combines all three chords we've covered, plus rests. By now, your child should be developing some good practice habits, so putting three chords all together to play a song should be an attainable goal. If you haven't already, it's a good time to start singing "Skip to My Lou" around the house—you'll be playing it next! Have fun!

Introducing the Page

Together, begin by slowly playing each of the three chords—C, C^7, and F—and discuss the different finger positions used to play them.

1. Since we must stay clear of the adjacent string to play an F chord, finger 1 needs to stand up nice and straight on the left side of the tip of the finger.

2. For the C^7 chord, finger 1 is probably not standing up quite as straight, but we are still on the left side of the very tip of the finger.

3. For the C chord, we are right up on the center of the tip of finger 3, making an "okay" sign.

4. Now, discuss the content of the "Remember" box on page 29—you'll have to take things slowly since "Rain Comes Down" features three chords, quarter rests, and chords that change in almost every measure.

5. Can your child find the ONE measure in "Rain Comes Down" that does NOT have a chord change?

6. Ask your child to find the ONE measure in "Rain Comes Down" that does NOT have a quarter rest.

7. Point out that the second line of music does not have a new chord frame at the beginning of the staff, so the F chord from the first line just continues.

Practice Suggestions

1. Point at each quarter-note slash and rest in "Rain Comes Down" as you slowly and evenly count aloud, saying "1 2 3 rest 1 2 3 rest." Take special note of the one measure where there is no rest.

2. Practice going from measure 1 into measure 2 several times—F to C is a new chord change.

3. Use the rests as an opportunity to move a finger to the next chord.

4. Counting aloud, slowly strum "Rain Comes Down."

5. When strumming this song is comfortable and easy, try playing along with Track 14.

Subsequent Lessons

Remember to stay vigilant about your child's playing position. Are their shoulders level and relaxed? Is their spine straight? Is their left arm hanging loosely in and not poking out to the left? Keep your child's foundation solid!

Three Chords in One Song

F **C⁷** **C**

Rain Comes Down

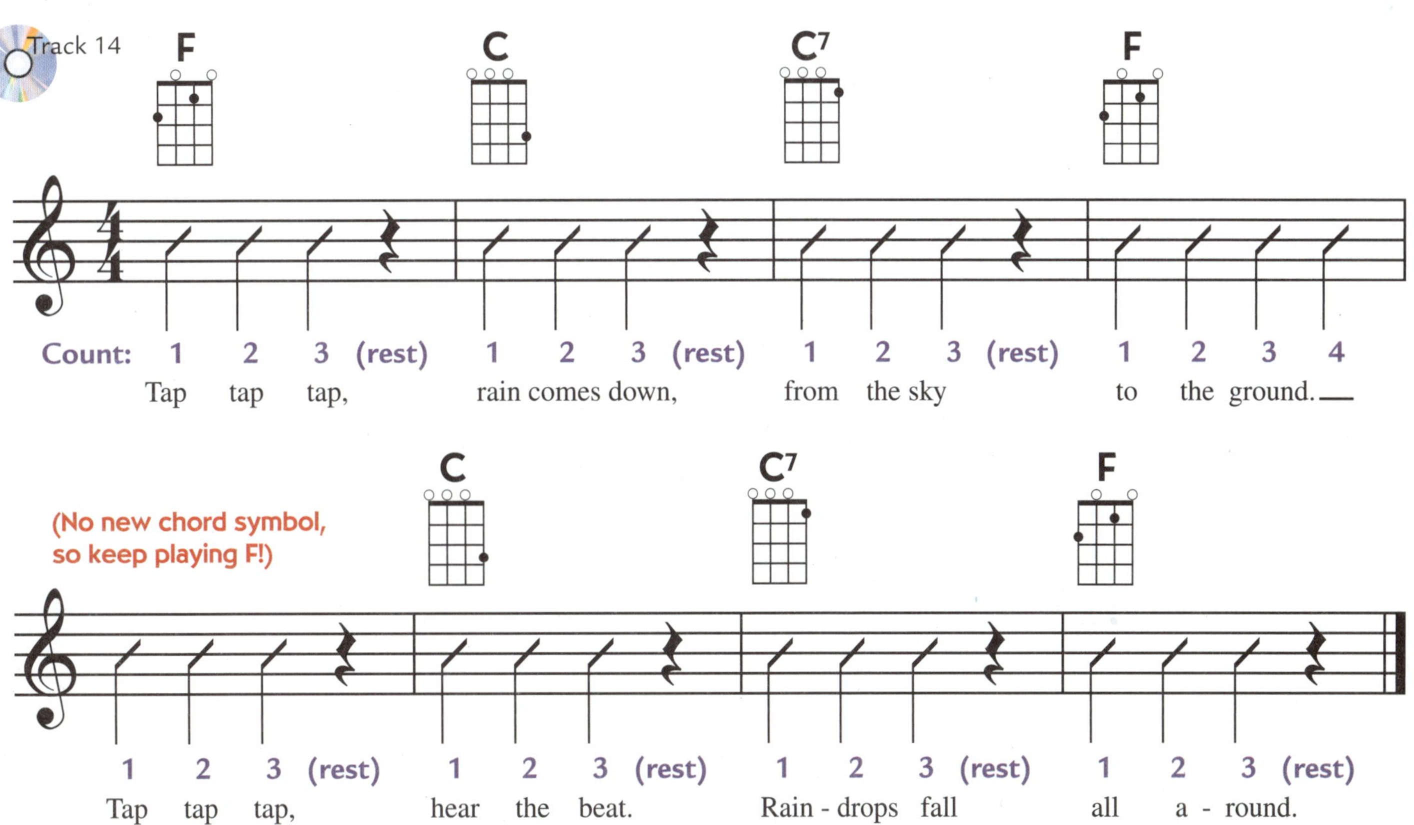

Skip to My Lou

It's time to strum along with this classic children's song on the ukulele! "Skip to My Lou" will provide further reinforcement of your child's ukulele skills and knowledge. This time, though, there is no rest between the C^7 and F chords, which takes us to the next level. In the meantime, now is a good time to start singing "London Bridge" around the house (it's the next lesson!). Try it in the car, next time you drive over a bridge!

Introducing the Page

1. Review the music with your child, pointing out the last two measures and the chord change without a rest between the chords.

2. Without strumming, practice moving finger 1 from the 1st fret of the 1st string to the 2nd string, right next door, as described in the Practice Tip.

Practice Suggestions

1. Slowly and evenly point at each quarter-note slash and say the name of the chord, saying "rest" at the quarter rests.

2. Repeat this activity with your child.

3. As you slowly and evenly point at the quarter-note slashes and rests, say the lyrics to the song, demonstrating how the words fall against the beats.

4. Repeat this activity with your child.

5. As you tap the beats on your lap, say the lyrics to the song in rhythm as your child practices the left hand without strumming.

6. Repeat this activity, but have your child add in the strumming.

Subsequent Lessons

Think about how many skills your child is combining to strum "Skip to My Lou": strumming in time, using the rest position to perform the quarter rests, keeping finger 1 clear of the 1st string to play an F chord, changing directly from a C^7 chord to an F chord without a rest in between, and maintaining a good position with the hands and ukulele, all at the same time!

That is a lot to coordinate! Plus, they may still be experiencing some discomfort when pressing down the strings with a left-hand finger. Be patient and encouraging! This may take a while to master. As you move on to the next lessons, return to "Skip to My Lou" and try playing along with Track 15, to keep things fun and interesting.

Skip to My Lou

Practice Tip

To change quickly from C⁷ to F in the last two measures, move your 1st finger to the 2nd string—that's not very far—and then put your 2nd finger on the 4th string.

C^7

F

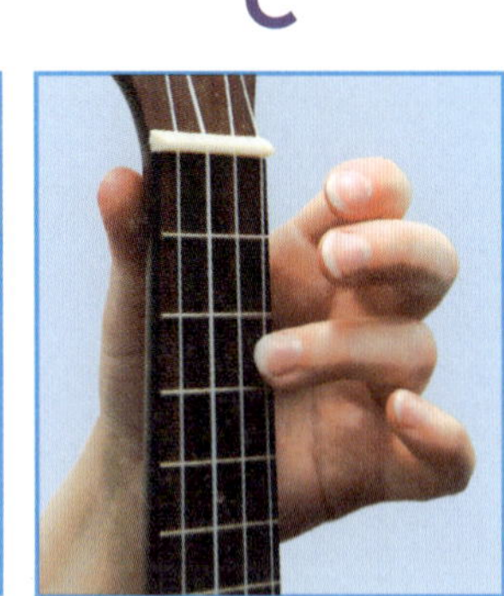

C

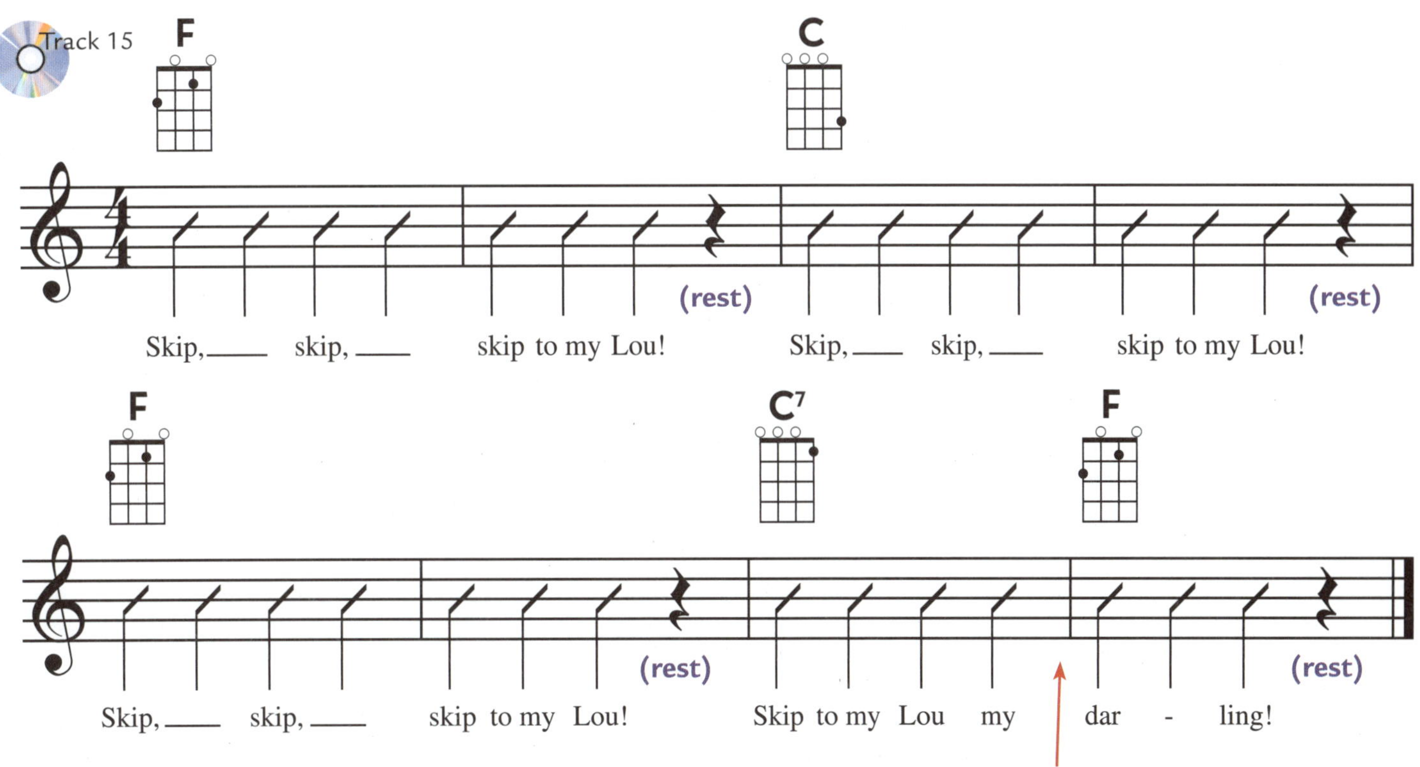

Remember to move your 1st finger to the 2nd string and then put your 2nd finger on the 4th string to play the F chord on the next beat.

London Bridge

Your child gets some more mileage out of all the skills they have learned with this fun song. There aren't any brand new skills here, so just enjoy adding another children's classic to your repertoire.

Introducing the Page

1. Review the music with your child, pointing out the last two measures and the chord change without a rest between the chords.

2. Point out that the second line of music does not have a new chord frame at the beginning of the staff, so the F chord from the first line just continues.

Practice Suggestions

1. Slowly and evenly point at each quarter-note slash and say the name of the chord, saying "rest" at the quarter rests.

2. Repeat this activity with your child.

3. As you slowly and evenly point at the quarter-note slashes and rests, say the lyrics to the song, demonstrating how the words fall against the beats.

4. Repeat this activity with your child.

5. As you tap the beats on your lap, say the lyrics to the song in rhythm as your child practices the left hand without strumming.

6. Repeat this activity, but have your child add in the strumming.

Subsequent Lessons

Think about how many skills your child is combining to strum "London Bridge": strumming in time, keeping finger 1 clear of the 1st string to play an F chord, changing directly from a C^7 chord to an F chord without a rest in between, and maintaining a good position with the hands and ukulele—all in one tune!

Notes:

London Bridge

The Repeat Sign

The left-facing *repeat sign* simply tells us to go back to the beginning and play again. In this case, when we perform "Merrily We Roll Along," we get to play it twice!

Introducing the Page

Show your child the repeat sign, and explain that it means to go back to the beginning and play again *without any break in the counting*. This is a good opportunity to mention that musicians try to look ahead in the music as they play. Also, explain how the quarter rest on the last beat of measure 8 can be used to move his or her eyes to the beginning of the song and be ready to continue.

Practice Suggestions

1. Point at each quarter-note slash and quarter rest in "Merrily We Roll Along" as you slowly and evenly count aloud, saying "1 2 3 4 1 2 3 rest," etc. When you come to the repeat, it's very important to keep the beat absolutely steady as you go from pointing at the quarter rest on the last beat to pointing at the quarter-note slash on the first beat.

2. Now, do this activity together with your child.

3. Practice playing measures 7 and 8 into measure 1 several times, focusing on keeping a steady beat.

4. Once that feels comfortable, play the whole song and have fun!

5. Together, play along with Track 17.

Subsequent Lessons

Remind your child not to squeeze the notes too hard. Here's a fun trick to try.

1. Cut a small piece of paper off of a larger sheet. Your piece should be about two inches long and half an inch wide.

2. Have your child put his or her 3rd finger down on the 1st string at the 3rd fret, to play a C chord.

3. Do the Butterfly Finger Exercise from page 16.

4. Now, while your child keeps the 3rd finger on its note, freely strumming the C chord, slip your piece of paper under the string. Yes! You should be able to move the paper freely under the finger without affecting the sound of the chord! The string should *not* be touching the wood of the fretboard!

Notes:

The Repeat Sign

Merrily We Roll Along

Love Somebody

Learning to play "Love Somebody" is another opportunity for your child to use all three chords—F, C^7, and C—the rest position, and the repeat sign.

Introducing the Page

1. Point out that in this song there are actually two different *verses*! The verse is the main part of a song and often tells a story. When two or more sections of a song have essentially the same music but different lyrics, each of these sections is considered one verse. The first time through the song, we sing the top line of lyrics shown under the music. When we repeat and play it a second time, we sing the second line of lyrics.

2. Look the song over with your child and have them say everything they observe about the music. Do they mention the repeat sign? The three different chords? The rest in measure 8? Make sure they have observed everything before continuing.

Practice Suggestions

1. Slowly and evenly point at each quarter-note slash and say the name of the chord, saying "rest" at the quarter rests.

2. Repeat this activity with your child.

3. As you slowly and evenly point at the quarter-note slashes and rests, say the lyrics to the song, demonstrating how the words fall against the beats, and keep a steady beat as you return to the beginning for the repeat.

4. Repeat this activity with your child.

5. As you tap the beats on your lap, speak the lyrics to the song in rhythm, saying the top line the first time through and the bottom line on the repeat.

6. Repeat this activity with your child.

7. Now, you sing the lyrics as your child strums the chords.

Subsequent Lessons

1. It's important for your child to develop the habit of looking over a piece of music before beginning to practice. What is the time signature? What chords are used? Are there rests? Is there a repeat sign? The more we know about a piece before we play, the easier and more fun it is to learn!

2. Together, play along with Track 18.

Notes:

Love Somebody

The G^7 Chord

So far, your child has learned three chords (C, C^7, and F) and used two fingers (1 and 2). Now, it's time to use three fingers to play a bluesy new chord: G^7.

Introducing the Page

Demonstrate the G^7 chord for your child.

1. Start with finger 1 positioned as if for an F chord, with finger 1 on the 2nd string at the 1st fret.

2. Keeping your left elbow still and very slightly rotating your forearm counterclockwise so that your pinky moves a little farther from the fretboard, add finger 2 to the 3rd string directly next to the 2nd fret. Make sure it is not bumping into the 2nd string. Use the very tip of the finger.

3. Add your 3rd finger to the 1st string, also directly next to the 2nd fret.

4. Making sure all three fingers are right next to their frets, strum all four strings. The top three strings should ring out clearly.

5. Together, listen to Track 19.

6. Repeat steps 1–4 with your child.

Practice Suggestions

1. Point at each quarter-note slash in "My Fourth Chord" as you slowly and evenly count aloud, saying "1 2 3 4 1 2 3 4."

2. Counting aloud, slowly strum "My Fourth Chord."

3. When strumming this song is comfortable and easy, try playing along with Track 20.

Subsequent Lessons

Because the G^7 chord requires the use of three fingers at once, it may feel more difficult than the first three chords covered in this book. Continue to remind your child not to squeeze too hard with any finger. Try the Butterfly Finger Exercise with all three fingers at once. Your child should just place them all in position for the chord without any pressure, and then strum, slowly adding pressure until all three strings ring clearly. Remember to be sensitive to potential discomfort and keep practice sessions short. It's important to avoid frustration. Take breaks and review past songs until they are comfortable with the G^7 chord and ready to move ahead.

Notes:

The G⁷ Chord

Use finger 1 to press the 2nd string at the 1st fret. Use fingers 2 and 3 to press the 3rd and 1st strings at the 2nd fret.

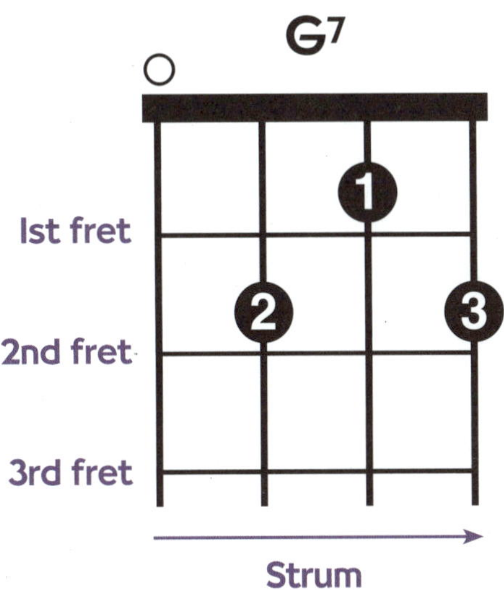

My Fourth Chord

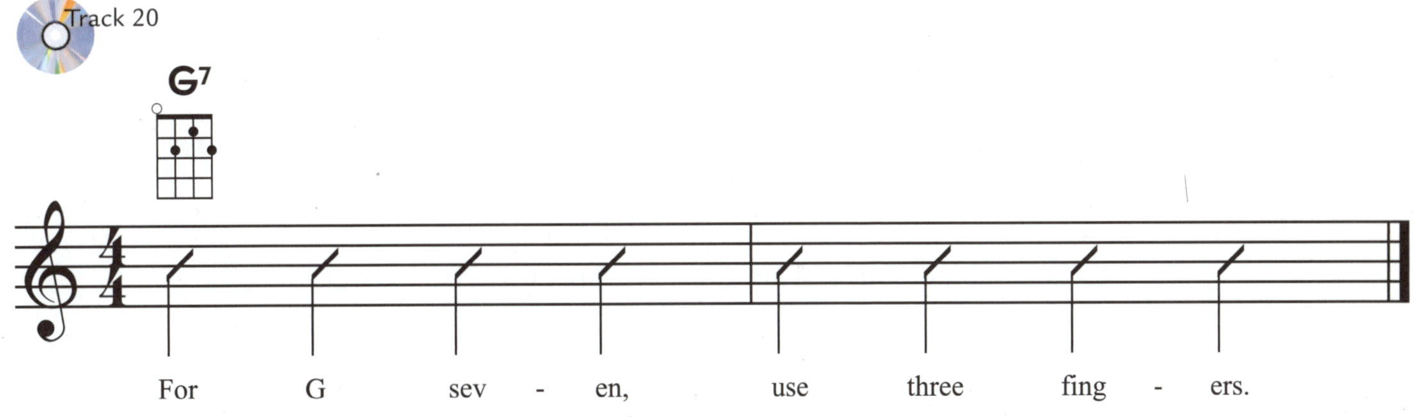

Using G^7 with Other Chords

This page gives your child the opportunity become accustomed to switching between G^7 and the other chords. There are three exercises, and together they cover the following chord changes: C to G^7, G^7 to C, F to G^7, G^7 to F, C to C^7, and C^7 to F. The secret to changing smoothly between chords is to observe the fingers they have in common and plan the most efficient finger movement between them.

Introducing the Page

Using the instructions below, demonstrate each chord change to your child, emphasizing the need for slow, direct finger movements. With a little planning, switching chords is easy! Show each chord individually, and then how to do each chord change called for in the three exercises. Allow them to master each chord change before playing the exercises.

Practice Suggestions

Exercise No. 1 covers the switches C to G^7 and G^7 to C. *Both chords use finger 3 on the 1st string.*

1. After strumming the C chord, release all pressure from finger 3, but *keep it in contact with the string*. Just lightly slide it from the 3rd fret down to the 2nd fret, as you place fingers 1 and 2 on their respective strings and frets for the G7 chord. Strum all four strings.

2. After strumming the G^7 chord, release all pressure from the fingers, but keep finger 3 in contact with the 1st string. Just lightly slide it from the 2nd fret up to the 3rd fret for the C chord. Strum.

Exercise No. 2 covers the switches of F to G^7 and G^7 to F. *Both chords use finger 1 on the 2nd string at the 1st fret.*

1. After strumming the F chord, keep light pressure on finger 1 as, for the G^7 chord, you slightly rotate the forearm counterclockwise and place fingers 2 and 3 on the 3rd and 1st strings, respectively, both directly next to the 2nd fret. Strum.

2. After strumming the G^7 chord, release fingers 2 and 3 from their strings, and then slightly rotate the forearm clockwise, place the 2nd finger on the 4th string and make sure your 1st finger is standing up on its tip on the 2nd string at the 1st fret so the 1st string can ring clearly as you strum the F chord.

Exercise No. 3 covers the switches F to G^7, G^7 to C, C to C^7, and C^7 to F. To review switching from F to G^7, see the notes for Exercise No. 2, above. To review switching from G^7 to C, see the notes for Exercise No. 1, above.

1. To switch from C to C^7, simply release finger 3 from the 1st string at the 3rd fret as you place finger 1 on the same string at the 1st fret.

2. To switch from C^7 to F, just release the pressure from the 1st finger on the 1st string and move it directly to the same fret on the 2nd string. Do this by lifting the finger just slightly—it should be a very small movement. Then add the 2nd finger to the 4th string at the 2nd fret.

Using G⁷ with Other Chords

Practice Tip

Before you play "A-Tisket, A-Tasket," "Aloha 'Oe," "When the Saints Go Marching In," and "Yankee Doodle," practice the exercises on this page. They will help you to change chords easily.

Play each exercise very slowly at first, and gradually play them faster. Don't move on to play the songs until you can easily move from chord to chord without missing a beat.

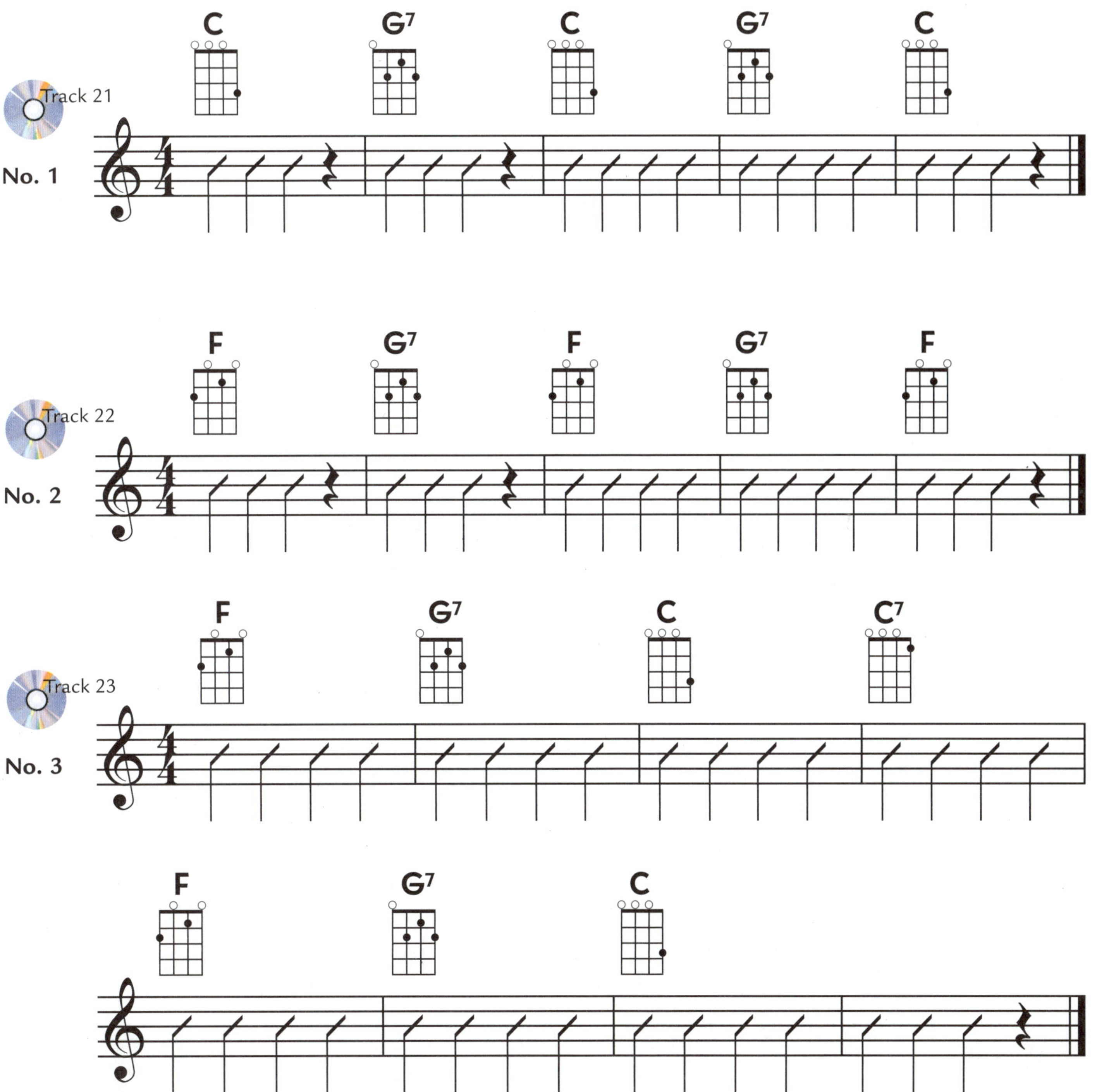

A-Tiskit, A-Tasket

"A-Tisket, A-Tasket" is a fun song to play using just the C and G^7 chords. Enjoy!

Introducing the Page

1. Review the music with your child, pointing out that there are no rests between the chords, and that only C and G^7 are used.

2. Remind your child that when no new chord appears at the beginning of a line, the previous chord is continued.

3. Point out that the song starts with three quarter-note rests. The first strum in the song is on beat 4 of the first measure.

Practice Suggestions

1. Together with your child, slowly tap the beats, point at the chord slashes, and count through the song while they finger the chords with their left hand, without strumming.

2. Together, practice slowly playing the song, while you sing, until it is easy.

3. When you're both ready, try it a little faster.

4. Repeat this activity, but have your child sing along.

Notes:

A-Tisket, A-Tasket

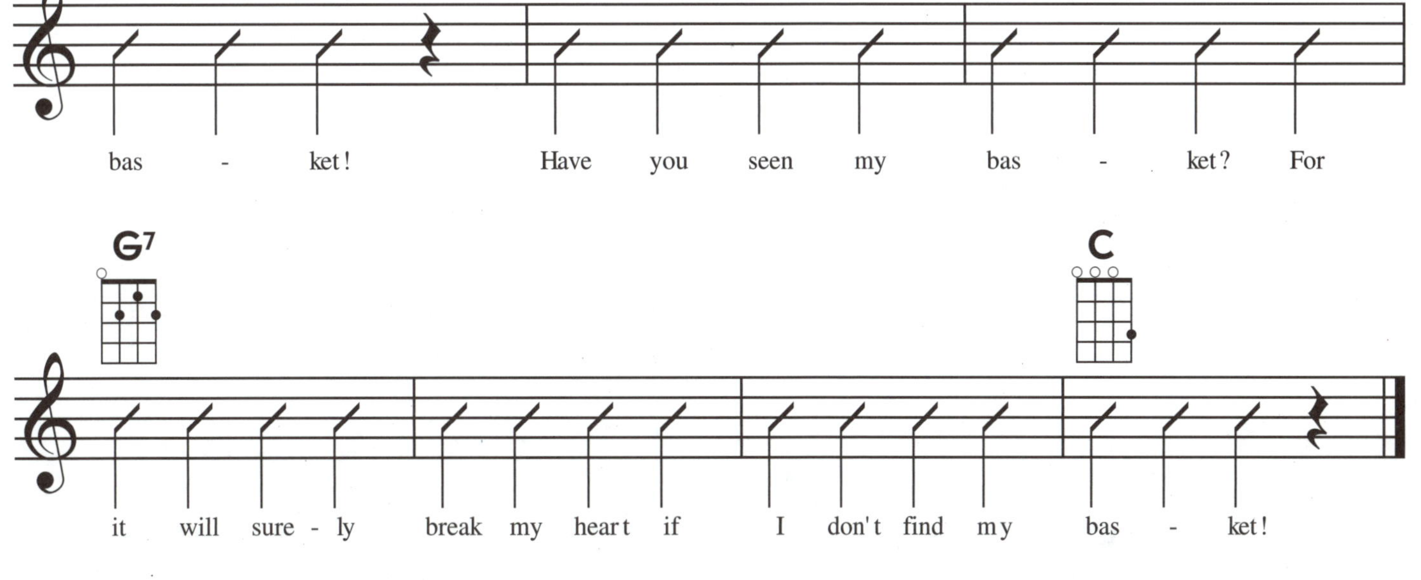

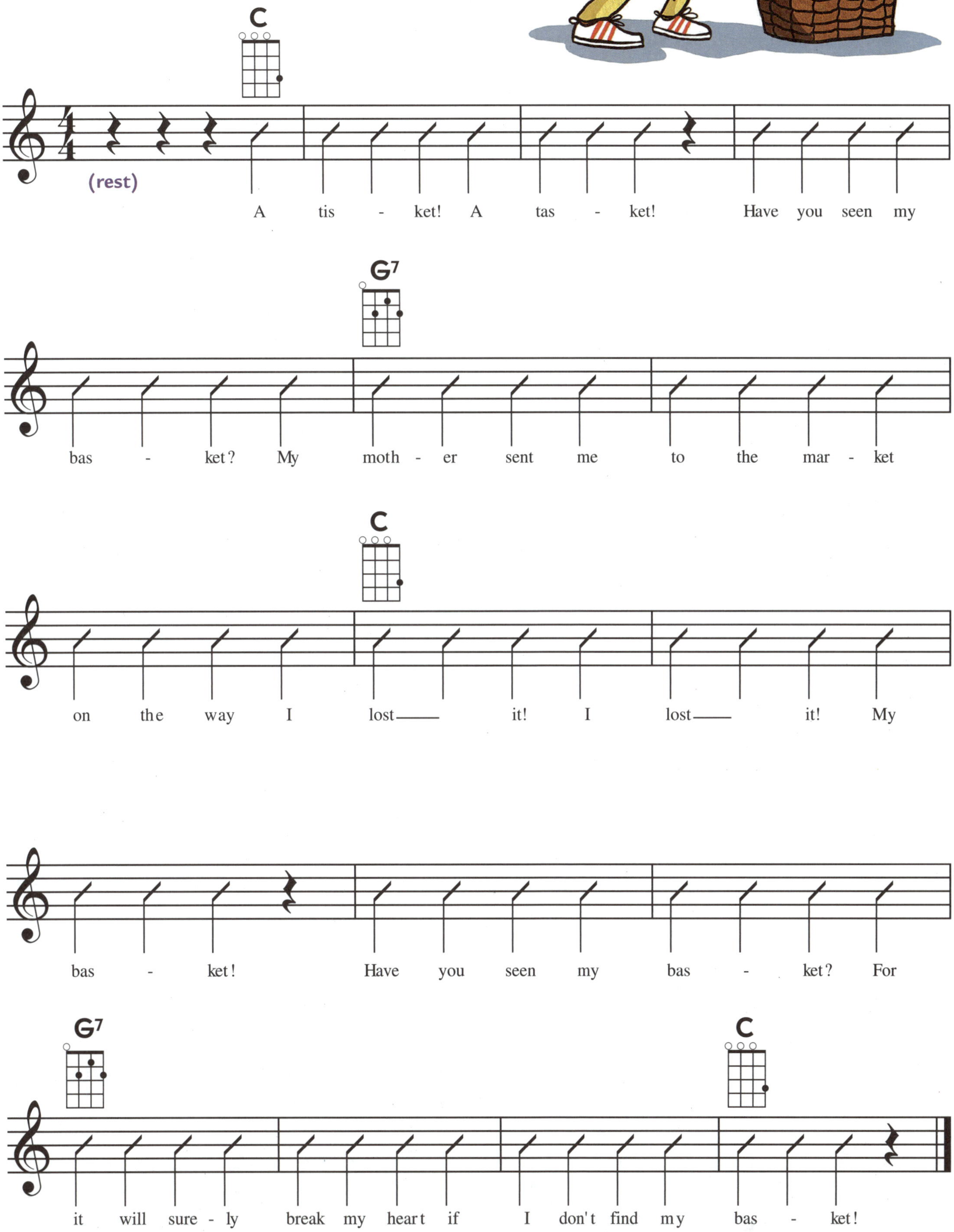

Aloha 'Oe (Farewell to Thee)

This famous Hawaiian song is a favorite among ukulele enthusiasts. It uses the F, C, C^7, and G^7 chords.

Introducing the Page

1. Point out that, like "A-Tisket, A-Tasket," this song starts with three quarter rests and a strum on beat 4 of the first measure.

2. Review the music with your child and identify every important element: the time signature, the rests, and the chords.

3. Remind your child that when no new chord appears at the beginning of a line, the previous chord is continued.

Practice Suggestions

1. Look for every chord change. Have your child try each one: F to C, C to G^7, G^7 to C, C to C^7, C^7 to F, and F to C. When it is easy for them to smoothly perform all of these chord changes, they are ready to play "Aloha 'Oe."

2. Together, practice slowly playing the song, and if you know this melody, sing along. Do this until it is easy for your child to play.

3. When you're both ready, try it a little faster.

4. Try playing along with track 25.

Notes:

Aloha ʻOe (Farewell to Thee)

Track 25

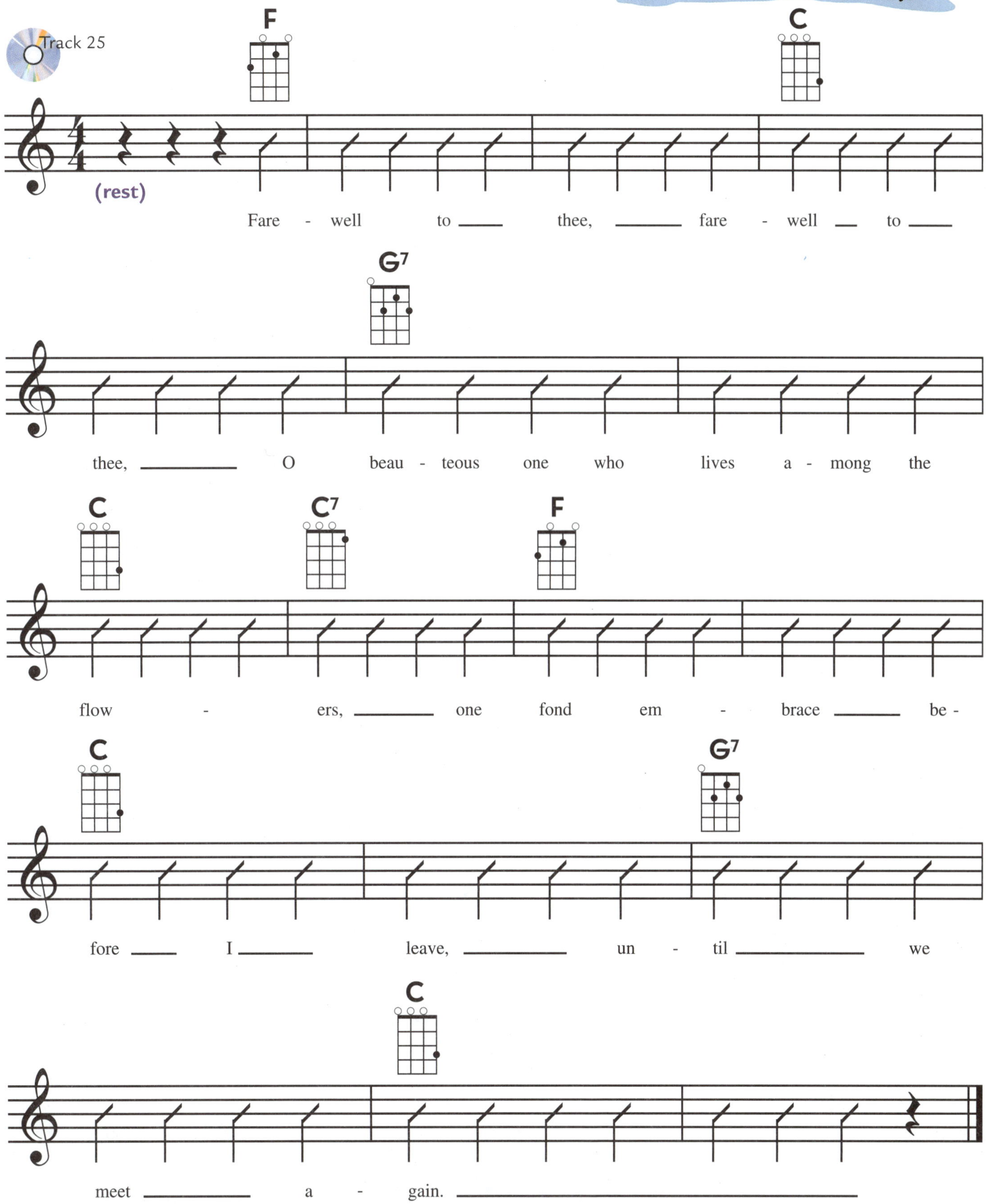

When the Saints Go Marching In

This song has a rest on the first beat. It features the chord changes C to G^7, G^7 to C, C to C^7, C^7 to F, and F to C.

Introducing the Page

If you spent adequate time mastering Exercises No. 1, 2, and 3 on page 41, your child will enjoy playing this fun song with little effort. Just remind them about the need for small, direct movements of the fingers and not to over-squeeze the strings. Encourage a light touch at all times.

It might be fun to talk about the song's roots in American gospel music, and its association with Dixieland jazz and the city of New Orleans.

Practice Suggestions

1. Try each chord change before beginning to play the song in rhythm. Make sure each change is clear in your child's mind and thus securely "under the fingers."

2. Count off one full measure before playing, making sure the student is ready to begin playing on the second beat instead of the first.

3. Tap out the beat on your lap as you sing and your child strums.

4. When the student is ready, try playing along with Track 26.

Subsequent Lessons

It will be fun for your child to try singing while they play. Singing requires that they be very secure with playing the chords, so it's a good idea to wait a couple of weeks, after the song has matured a bit. It's important to stay with a song for a little while, rather than putting it down as soon as it's learned. It is, however, a bit of a balancing act because the child can become discouraged if they don't feel like they're "moving on." You know your child better than anyone! Keep your finger on the pulse of their enthusiasm and keep it high!

Notes:

When the Saints Go Marching In

Yankee Doodle

Nowadays, this fun song is considered patriotic, but your child may enjoy knowing that, originally, "doodle" was a word used to describe a silly person. It wasn't very nice! The song features the chord changes C to G^7, G^7 to C, C to F, F to G^7, C to G, and F to C.

Introducing the Page

As with "When the Saints," if your child is properly prepared, this will be a fun song to play.

1. Point out the change from G^7 to C going from measure 2 to measure 3; there are only two strums and then the chord changes. This is a great example of how it helps to look closely at the music before playing. Practice measures 1–3 several times before playing the whole song.

2. Point out the four rests in this song. They don't happen at obvious, regular intervals, so make sure your child is aware of them.

Practice Suggestions

1. Try each chord change before beginning to play the song in rhythm. Make sure each change is clear in your child's mind and thus securely "under the fingers."

2. Tap out the beat on your lap as you sing and your child strums.

3. When the student is ready, try playing along with Track 27.

Subsequent Lessons

Always look for opportunities to turn potential tricky spots into exercises for your child to master before beginning to play a song. Taken out of context, these spots can be easier to learn, and this will take the stress out of overcoming challenges some songs may present. That's what we did above with measures 1–3 of this song. Just like carefully looking over the music before beginning to play, this kind of preparation can make learning to play ukulele easier for your child.

As your child's ukulele teacher, it is always best to be prepared for the lessons. If you are new to the ukulele too, be sure to become comfortable with the material yourself before introducing it to your child.

Notes:

Yankee Doodle

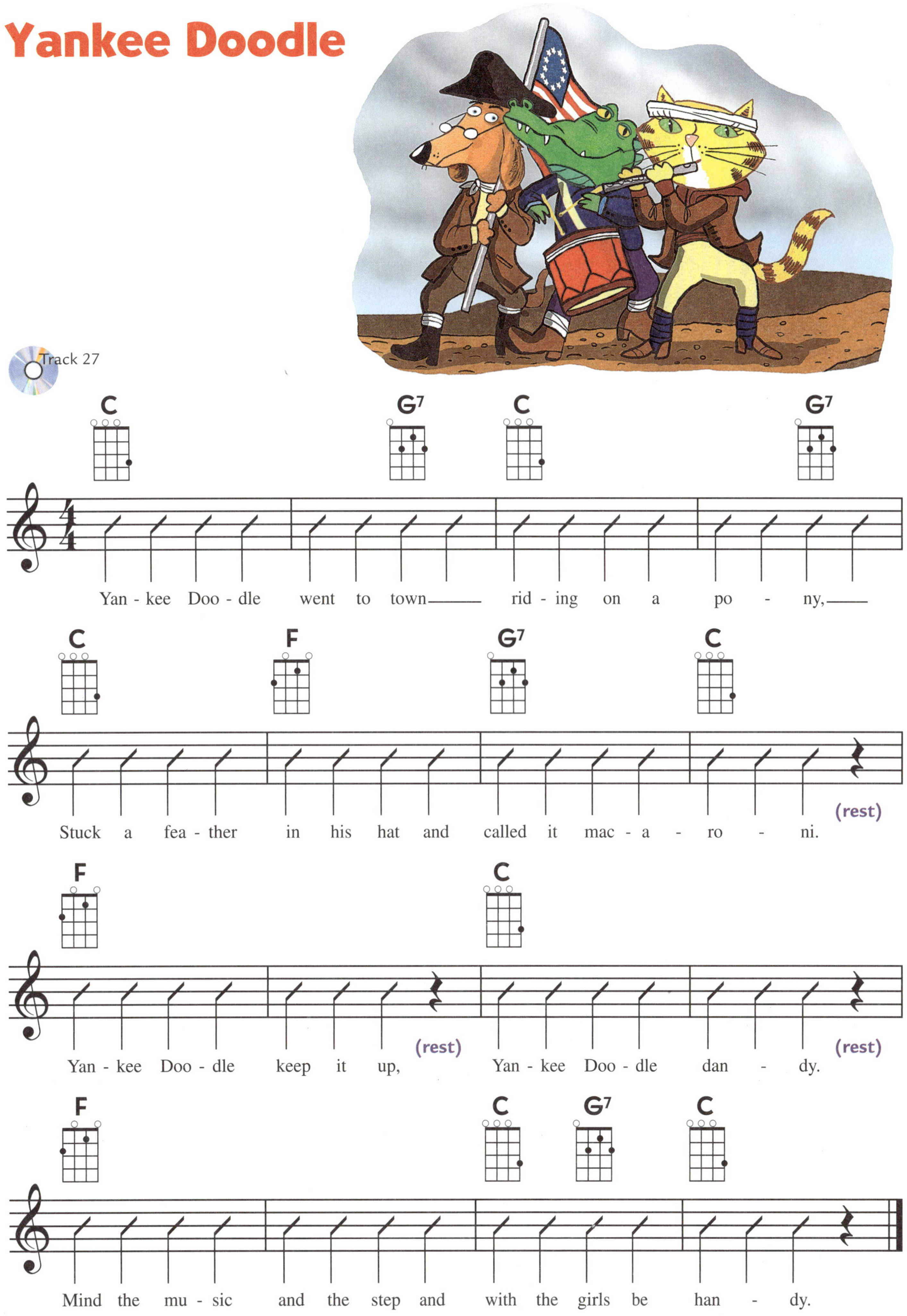

C   G⁷   C   G⁷

Yan - kee Doo - dle went to town——— rid - ing on a po - ny,———

C   F   G⁷   C

Stuck a fea - ther in his hat and called it mac - a - ro - ni. *(rest)*

F   C

Yan - kee Doo - dle keep it up, *(rest)* Yan - kee Doo - dle dan - dy. *(rest)*

F   C G⁷ C

Mind the mu - sic and the step and with the girls be han - dy.

49

Getting Acquainted with Music Notation

Learning to read music notation will enable your child to read and play melodies on the ukulele. This is a skill they will be able to use the rest of their life.

Introducing the Page

Review the material on page 51 with your child. Make sure they understand that:

1. Musical sounds are represented by *notes*.

2. Each kind of note looks different (discuss black notes, white notes, stems, and flags), and each lasts a different amount of time.

3. The time a note lasts is called its *note value*.

4. Notes and rests are written on a *staff*, the lines and spaces of which are numbered from the bottom up.

5. Where a note appears on a staff determines its note name.

6. Note names come from the music alphabet, which is easy to learn because it has only seven letters: A B C D E F G.

7. Ukulele music uses a *G clef*, often called the *treble clef*.

Practice Suggestions

For a few moments, skip ahead in the book to "Mary Had a Little Lamb" on page 89. Together, observe:

1. The combination of black notes and white notes.

2. Some notes are on lines, some are in spaces.

3. There are some chord strums mixed in with the melody notes.

Subsequent Lessons

As you move forward in the book, new notes and different time values will be introduced. Music is both an aural and a written language, and kids are *great* at learning new languages! The younger your child is, the more natural it is for them to learn a language, but try to be sensitive to the pace of learning. Make sure the student is *really reading the music* and *not* playing strictly by ear. Being able to play by ear is a true gift, but it should never get in the way of becoming a literate musician.

Notes:

Getting Acquainted with Music Notation

Notes

Musical sounds are represented by symbols called *notes*. Their time value is determined by their color (black or white), and by stems and flags attached to them.

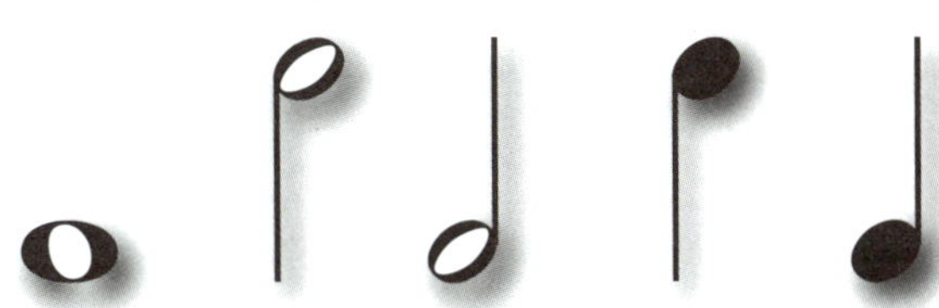

The Staff

Each note has a name. That name depends on where the note is found on the *staff*. The staff is made up of five horizontal lines and the spaces between those lines.

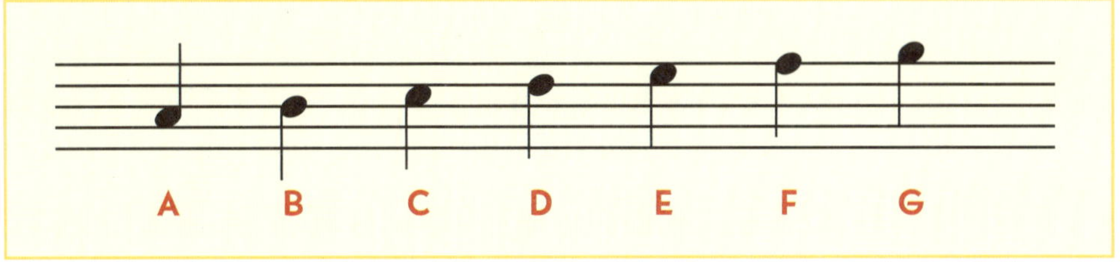

The Music Alphabet

The notes are named after the first seven letters of the alphabet (A–G).

Clefs

As music notation progressed through history, the staff had from two to twenty lines, and symbols were invented that would always give you a reference point for all the other notes. These symbols were called *clefs*.

Music for the ukulele is written in the *G* or *treble clef*. Originally, the Gothic letter G was used on a four-line staff to show the pitch G.

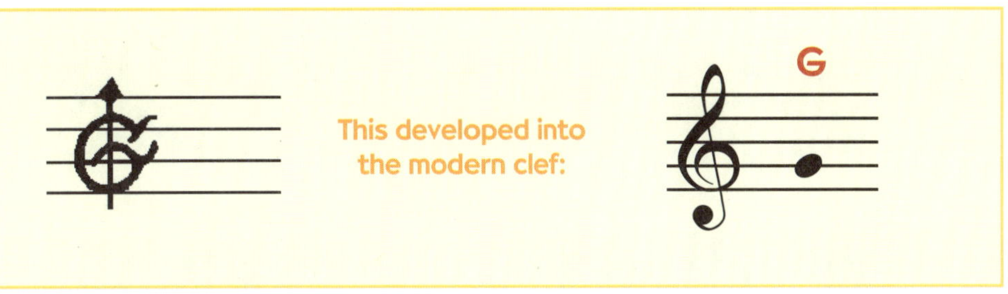

Getting Acquainted with Music Notation

It's time to start learning the names of the notes on the lines and spaces. The quarter note, which equals one beat, is also introduced.

Introducing the Page

Review the information on page 53 with your child.

1. Using the phrase **E**very **G**ood **B**ird **D**oes **F**ly makes it easy to learn the names of the notes on the lines, because from the bottom line up, they are E G B D F.

2. It might be fun for your child to make up his or her own phrase for learning the names of the notes on the lines.

3. The notes in the spaces, from the bottom up, form the word FACE.

4. Discuss the parts of the quarter note with your child, pointing out that it has a *stem* and the *note head* is black.

5. The chart showing the notes on the lines and spaces demonstrates how the stem of a quarter note can go up on the right side of the note head or down on the left side of the note head.

Practice Suggestions

1. Spend a little time making sure your child has learned the names of the notes on the lines and spaces.

2. Flip ahead in the book to page 75, and see if your child can point to the notes in "A-Choo!" and say their names. Flip back to page 51 and review as often as necessary.

3. Count aloud slowly, saying "1 2 3 4 1 2 3 4," etc., and point at the notes as you tap out on your lap the rhythms in "Clap and Count out Loud."

4. Now, point at the notes as your child counts with you and claps the rhythms in "Clap and Count out Loud."

Subsequent Lessons

Counting and clapping the rhythm should become an integral part of learning every new piece. This should become a habit and an important part of every practice session for years to come.

Notes:

An easy way to remember the notes on the lines is using the phrase
Every **G**ood **B**ird **D**oes **F**ly. Remembering the notes in the spaces is even
easier because they spell the word **FACE**, which rhymes with "space."

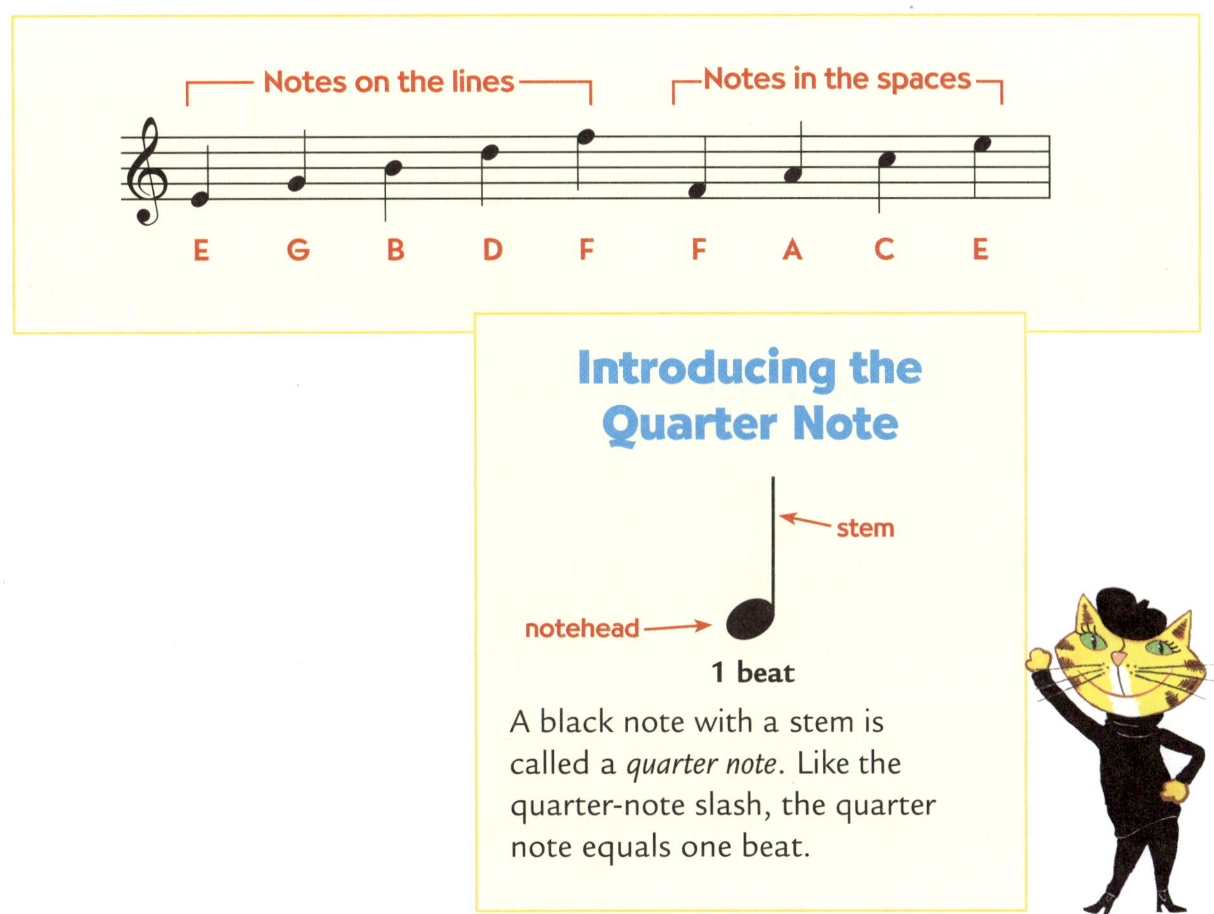

A black note with a stem is
called a *quarter note*. Like the
quarter-note slash, the quarter
note equals one beat.

Clap and Count out Loud

Notes on the First String: Introducing A

It's time for your child to become accustomed to picking a single string, as opposed to strumming four at once, as with the chords. This is an excellent time to review how to hold a pick, which is covered at the top of page 13. Make sure your child is holding it firmly but not squeezing too hard, and that just a small portion of the pick is sticking out below the thumb and index finger. We only use the very tip of the pick to strike a single string. If you use your finger to strum, use the same finger to pick individual notes in the same way as using a pick.

Introducing the Page

1. Review the information at the top of the page, pointing out that the names of the notes on the spaces spell the word "FACE" and the second space is called A.

2. Point out the circle (O) above the note head. This means to pick the *open* string, which is a string that is not being fingered with the left hand.

3. Direct your child to the fretboard diagram at the top right of the page; point out how strings that are not being played are represented with dotted lines and the string being played is a solid line.

4. Practice small *downpick* (toward the floor) with the pick or finger on the 1st string (the string closest to the floor).

5. Counting aloud slowly, demonstrate "Abby, the Armadillo" the exercise using only A notes at the bottom of the page.

6. Have your child play along with you, as he or she counts aloud.

Practice Suggestions

1. It's always a good idea to count off one complete measure before you or your child begin to play. This sets the pace and lets them know when to begin playing. Explain that you'll say "1 2 3 4" and then he or she should start playing on the next "1." Demonstrate.

2. Just for fun, try saying the lyrics of the song, shown below the staff, in rhythm with your child while he or she plays.

Subsequent Lessons

Review good practice habits with your child often. They should remember to always look over the music carefully before they play, noting the time signature, saying the names of the notes, counting and clapping the rhythms, taking special note of rests, identifying any potential tricky spots, etc. The more thorough and careful the practice sessions, the quicker we learn to play and the more fun we have!

Notes:

Introducing A

A note sitting on the second space of the treble clef staff is called A. To play this note, pick the open 1st string (meaning without putting a left-hand finger on it).

Abby, the Armadillo

Picking

- Play each A slowly and evenly, using a *downpick* motion. We will use only downpicks for the rest of the book.

- Use only a little motion to pick each note, just like strumming.

The Note A with Chords

On this page, your child will learn to combine single notes and three-note-chord strums.

Introducing the Page

1. It's a good idea to discuss the subtle difference between picking a single string and strumming a three-string chord. Your child should use a small downward motion to pick the A note on the open A string, and only a slightly larger motion to strum the chord. Both motions are small and done mostly from the wrist.

2. Discuss the F and C^7 chords, and how they are both played with finger 1 on the 1st fret. For the F chord, finger 1 is on the 2nd string; for the C^7 chord, it's on the 1st string. Changing chords requires a very small movement.

Practice Suggestions

1. Practice "Note and Strum Warm-up." Notice the repeat sign and the rests on beat 4 of each measure.

2. Play it until both the picks and strums are played with ease, confidence, and accuracy.

3. Look over the music for "Note and Strum." Observe all the elements: the picks, the strums, the rests, the chord changes, etc.

4. Together, slowly point at each note and say, as appropriate, the name of the note or chord being picked or strummed, like this: "Pick A, strum F, strum F, rest," etc.

5. Counting slowly, demonstrate by playing the piece.

6. Now, count slowly and play through the song together.

7. Finally, have your child play through the piece alone.

Subsequent Lessons

Strive to give your child more and more independence with their ukulele playing. It's very helpful for you to demonstrate each new concept and skill, and to play along with them, but the more the student can play on their own, the better!

Notes:

The Note A with Chords

F Chord   **C⁷ Chord**

Track 31

Note and Strum

Track 32

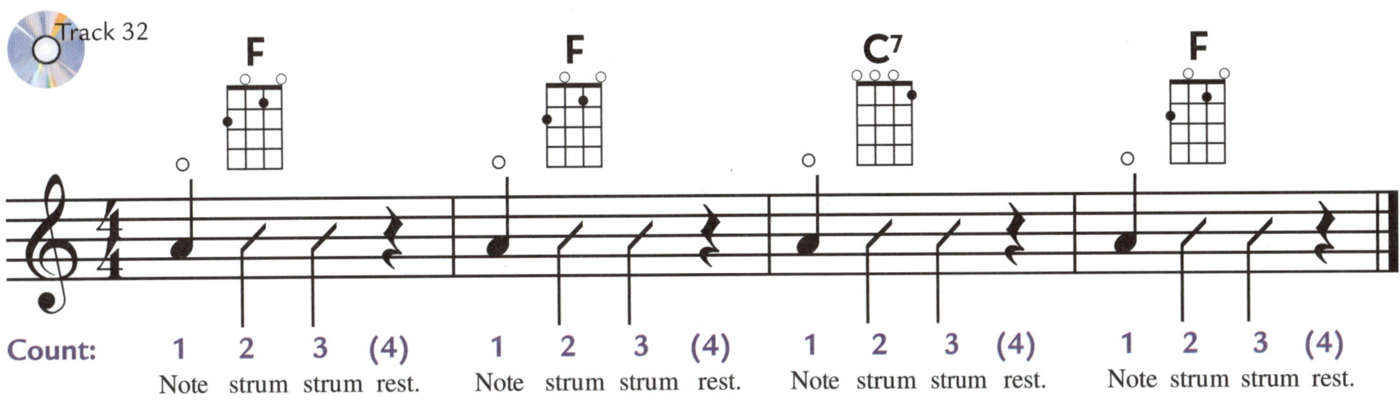

Notes on the First String: Introducing F

Remember "Every Good Bird Does Fly?" That's the phrase we used for memorizing the names of the notes on the staff, and "Bird" corresponds to the third line of the staff, so, a note placed on that line is called "B."

Introducing the Page

1. Review the information at the top of the page, reminding them that the names of the lines correspond to "Every Good Bird Does Fly," and the third line is called B.

2. Point out the number 2 above the note head. This means the 2nd finger is used to play the note.

3. Direct your child to the fretboard diagram at the top right of the page; point out how strings that are not being played are represented with dotted lines and the string being played is a solid line. The B note is on the 1st string at the 2nd fret.

Practice Suggestions

1. Practicing "Up-Down-Up Warm-up" will prepare your child to play the song.

2. Point at each note of "Up-Down-Up" and say the name of the note aloud.

3. Repeat this activity with your child.

4. Point at each note of "Up-Down-Up" and say the fingering aloud, saying "O" for "open" and "2" for the 2nd finger (for example, the first two measures are "O O O O 2 2 2 2").

5. Counting aloud slowly, demonstrate the tune.

6. Now, have your child play the tune while you slowly count together.

Subsequent Lessons

When learning to play single-note melodies, make pointing at notes and saying the finger numbers a part of your child's practice routine. The more clearly they know beforehand how the music is supposed to be played, the easier it will be to learn.

Notes:

Notes on the First String
Introducing B

A note on the middle line of the staff is called B. To play this note, use finger 2 to press the 1st string at the 2nd fret. Use a downpick motion to play only the 1st string.

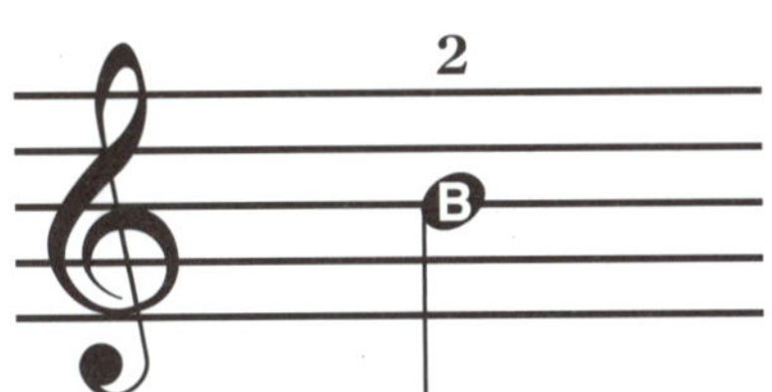

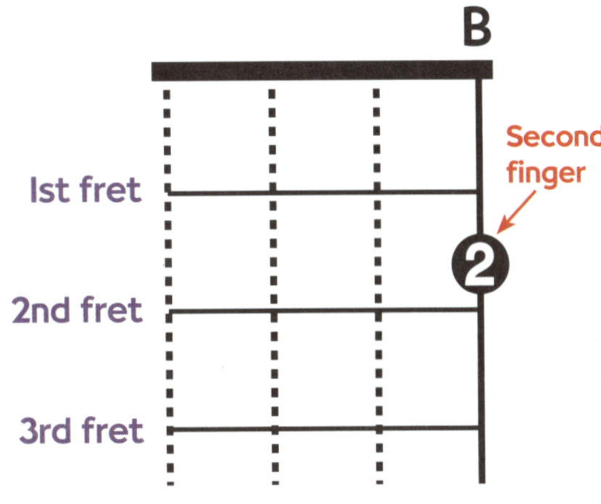

Up-Down-Up Warm-up

Before playing "Up-Down-Up," practice this exercise until you are comfortable playing the note B.

Up-Down-Up

The Notes A and B with Chords

This will be a fun and easy page because the left hand will have a simple job—moving from finger 2 at the 2nd fret to finger 3 at the 3rd fret, on the 1st string.

Introducing the Page

1. Review the Practice Tip with your child.

2. Show your child how they can have their fingers set for an F chord while they play the A note. The only difference between the left-hand positions for the note A note and the F chord should be how many strings are played with the pick. For the A, pick just the 1st string but have your fingers ready for the F chord. Then, for the F chord, strum all four strings.

3. Carefully look over the music with your child. Observe which notes are picked and which are strummed. Picked single notes are written with round note heads; chord strums are written with strum slash marks.

4. As you did on page 57, together, slowly point at each note and say, as appropriate, the name of the note or chord being picked or strummed, like this: "Pick A, strum F, strum F, rest," etc.

5. Repeat this activity with your child.

6. Together, count aloud and clap the rhythm, saying "1 2 3 rest," etc.

Practice Suggestions

1. Slowly counting aloud, pick and strum through the music.

2. Have your child play along with you. Make sure they leave finger 2 down when going from measure 2 to measure 3.

3. Let your child play through it alone.

Subsequent Lessons

1. Play the example as many as times as needed.

2. Play along with the recording.

Notes:

The Notes A and B with Chords

Practice Tip

For this tune, notice that the note B and the C chord are one finger apart. Finger the B with the 2nd finger on the 2nd fret of the 1st string, and then use the 3rd finger on the 3rd fret of the 1st string to play the C chord. First, just practice switching those fingers and then play the music below.

Note B

C Chord

Track 36

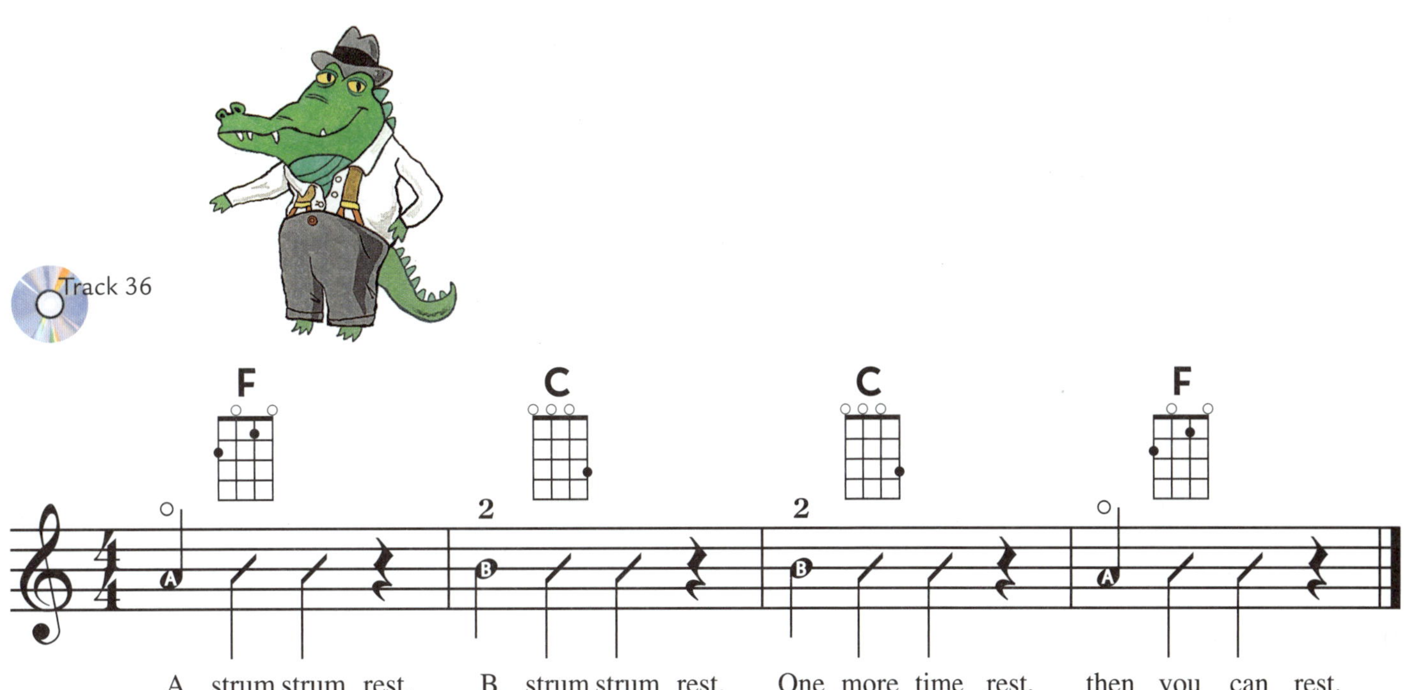

Notes on the First String: Introducing C

The note C sits on the third space in the staff (F–A–**C**–E). It is played with finger 3 at the 3rd fret of the 1st string.

Introducing the Page

1. Ask your child to play a C chord (review page 19, if necessary).

2. Now, ask him or her to keep their left hand in that position and pick just the 1st string, like they did to play the A and B notes. Congratulate your child for playing a new note!

3. Draw your child's attention to the picture of the C note on the staff, the fretboard diagram, and the photograph on page 63.

Practice Suggestions

1. Practicing "C Warm-up" will prepare your child to play "The Mountain Climber."

2. Point at each note of "The Mountain Climber" and say the name of the note aloud.

3. Repeat this activity with your child.

4. Point at each note and say the fingering aloud, saying "O" for "open," "2" for the 2nd finger, and "3" for the 3rd finger.

5. Counting aloud slowly, demonstrate the example.

6. Now, have your child play the example while you slowly count together.

Subsequent Lessons

The more notes and chords being used in a song, the more important it is for your child to have good practice habits. Make sure he or she always looks over the music, names the notes, names the fingers, counts and claps the rhythms, and plays slowly at first. Once your child can play a song exercise securely and confidently, let them play along with the recording.

Notes:

Introducing C

Hear this note!

Track 37

A note sitting on the third space of the treble clef staff is called C. Use finger 3 to press the 1st string at the 3rd fret. Use a downpick motion to play only the 1st string.

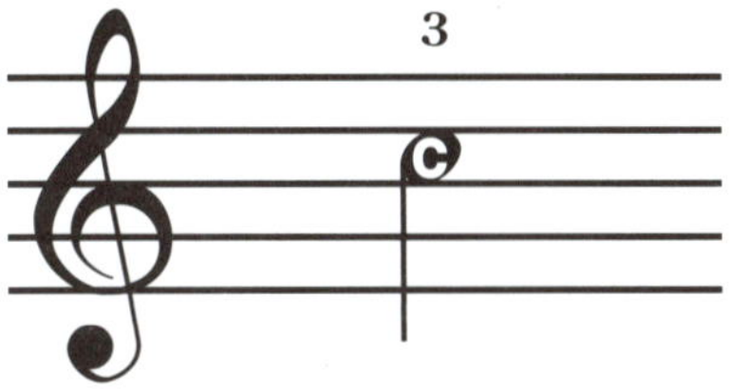

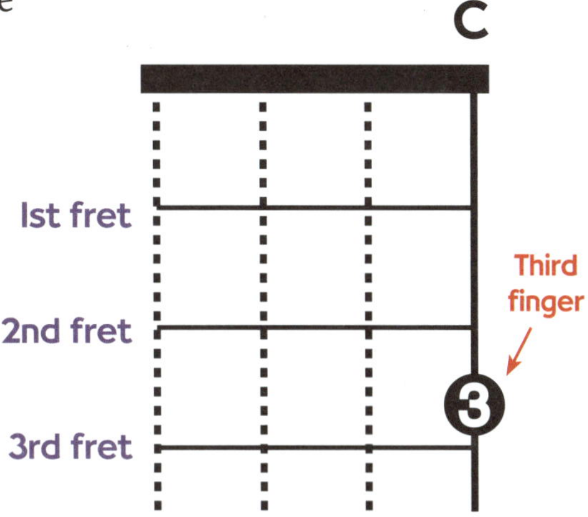

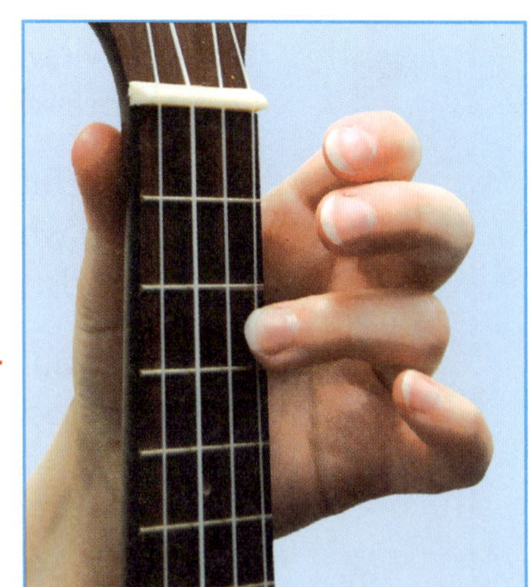

3
C

C
1st fret
2nd fret
3rd fret
Third finger
3

Track 38

C Warm-up

3
C

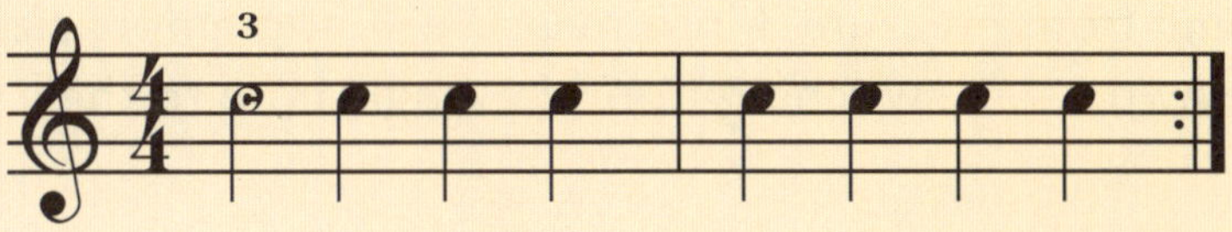

The Mountain Climber

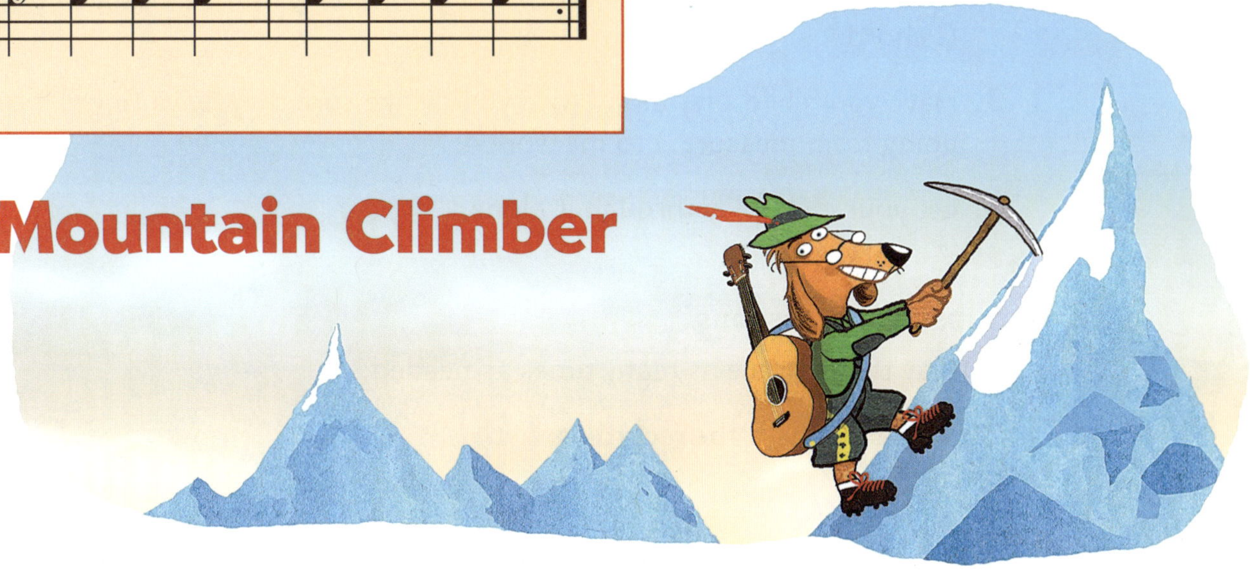

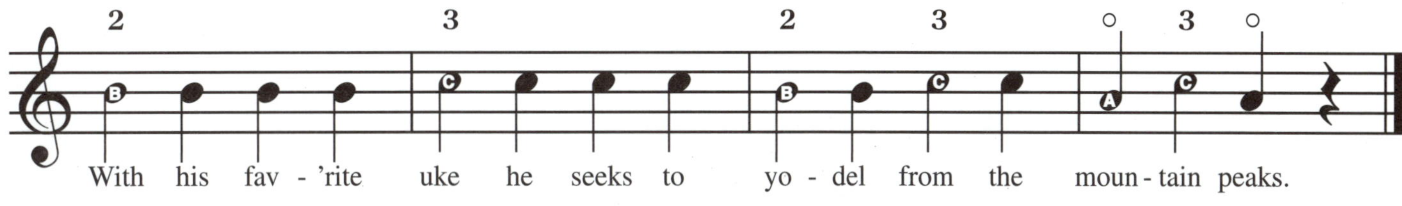

Track 39

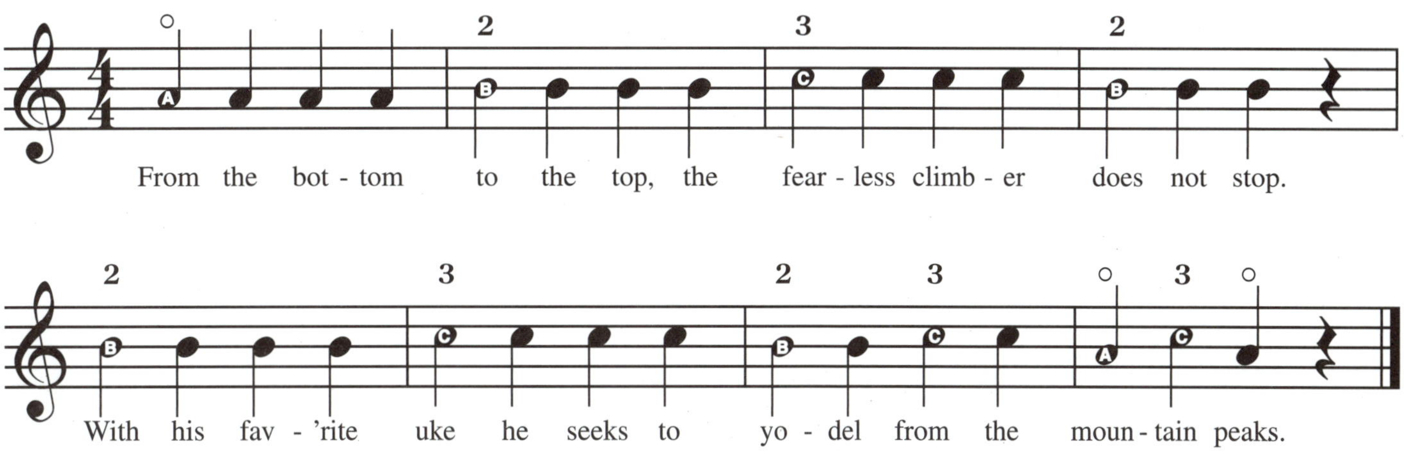

From the bot - tom to the top, the fear - less climb - er does not stop.
With his fav - 'rite uke he seeks to yo - del from the moun - tain peaks.

The Notes A, B, and C with Chords

The note C and the C chord are both fingered with finger 3 at the 3rd fret on the 1st string.

Introducing the Page

1. Review the practice tip with your child and remind them to hold finger 3 on its note when switching from the C note to the C chord.

2. Carefully look over the music with your child. Observe which notes are picked and which are strummed. Picked single notes are written with round note heads; chord strums are written with strum slash marks.

3. As you did on page 57, together, slowly point at each note and say, as appropriate, the name of the note or chord being picked or strummed.

4. Repeat this activity with your child.

5. Point out that "Brave in the Cave" has only quarter notes and quarter-note slashes; there are no rests.

Practice Suggestions

1. Slowly counting aloud, pick and strum through the music.

2. Make an exercise out of going from measure 3 into measure 4, and emphasize that the 3rd finger is held down when switching from the single note to the C chord.

3. Have your child play along with you. Make sure they leave finger 3 down when going from measure 3 to measure 4.

4. Let your child play through it alone.

Subsequent Lessons

1. Play the example as many times as needed.

2. Play along with the recording.

Notes:

The Notes A, B, and C with Chords

Practice Tip

Notice that the note C and the C chord are both fingered with finger 3 at the 3rd fret on the 1st string.

Note C

C Chord

Hold down the 3rd finger between the note C and the C chord.

Brave in the Cave

Track 40

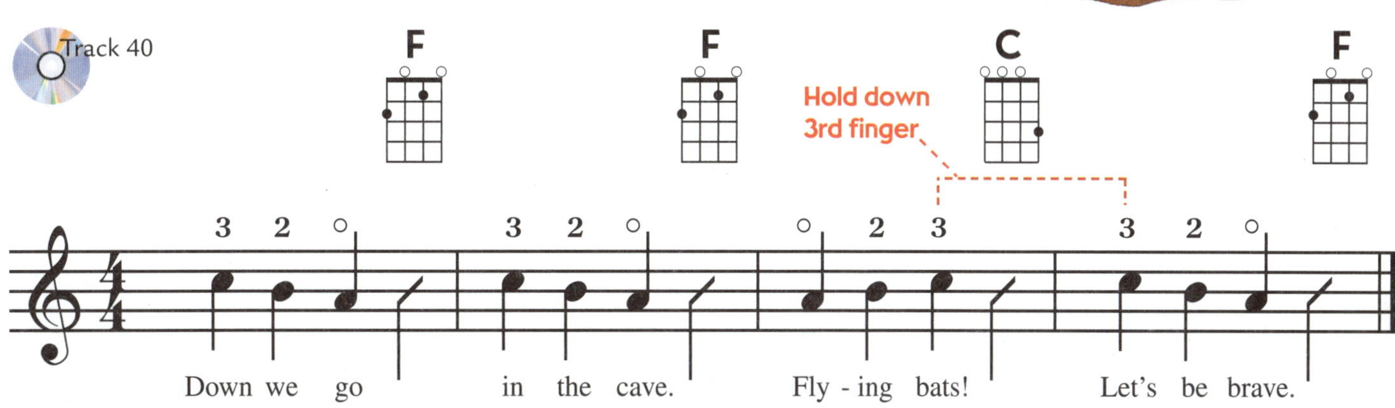

Notes on the Second String: Introducing E

A note on the lowest (first) line of the staff is called E, and it is played on the open 2nd string.

Introducing the Page

1. Since the 2nd string is an inside string (it's neither the closest to the ground nor the closest to the ceiling), playing it will take some getting used to. Until your child gets a "feel" for it, they may have to look at their right hand often, especially when the music calls for changing strings. Encourage them to keep their eyes on the music as soon as you can.

2. Draw your child's attention to the picture of the E note on the staff and the fretboard diagram on page 67.

3. "E Warm-up" will help your child prepare for "Two Open Strings" and "Two-String Melody." Note the repeat sign.

Practice Suggestions

For both songs:

1. Point at the notes and say their names.

2. Point at the notes and say the fingerings. Since there are two strings now, when naming the fingerings for the open strings, say "O 1st" or "O 2nd."

3. Demonstrate the song as your child counts aloud with you.

4. Have your child count and play with you.

5. Have your child count and play alone.

Subsequent Lessons

1. Continue practicing "Two Open Strings" and "Two-String Melody" as needed.

2. Play along with the recording.

Notes:

Introducing E

Hear this note!

Track 41

A note on the lowest line of the staff is called E. Play the 2nd string open.

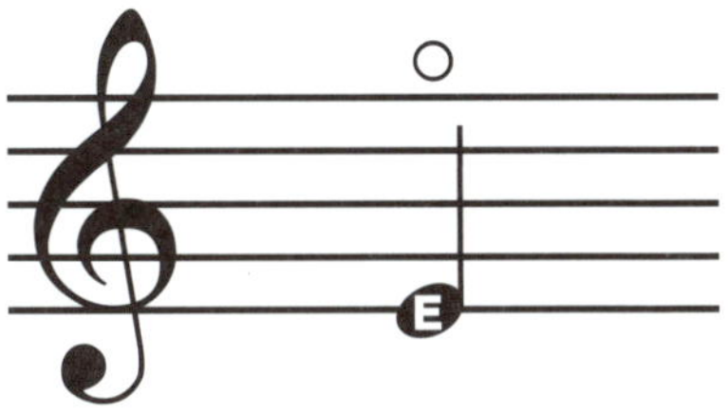

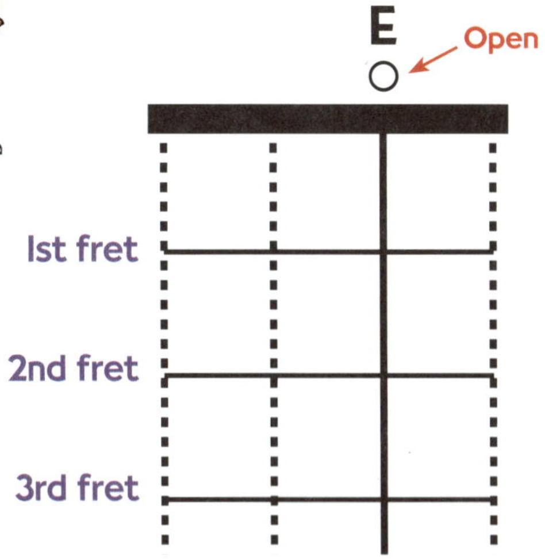

E ← Open

1st fret

2nd fret

3rd fret

Track 42

E Warm-up

Two Open Strings

Track 43

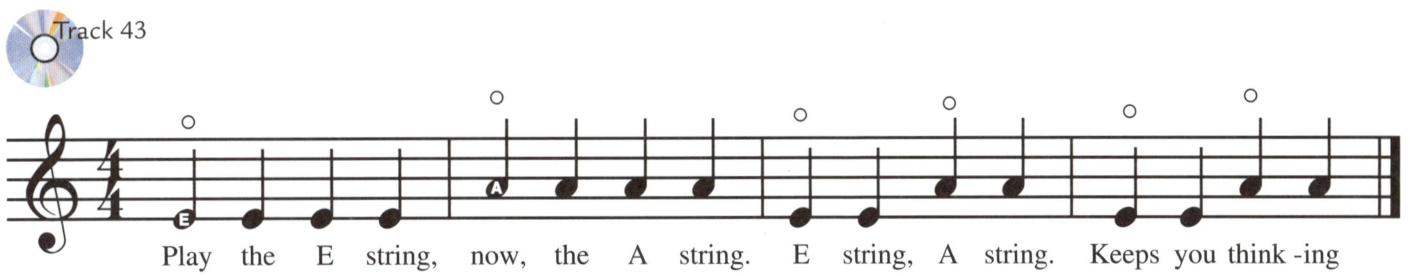

Two-String Melody

Track 44

Jumping Around

"Jumping Around" features switching between the 1st and 2nd strings, and the fingers 2 and 3.

Introducing the Page

1. Review the C^7 chord (page 23) and the C chord (page 19).

2. Without picking or strumming, put finger 1 in position for a C^7 chord (finger 1 on the 1st string, 1st fret) then switch to putting finger 3 in position for a C chord (finger 3 on the 1st string, 3rd fret). Switch back and forth between the two positions.

3. Add strumming to step 2. Strum all four strings.

4. Now, add picking the 1st string to step 2, instead of strumming.

5. Point out that measures 5 and 6 are exactly the same as measures 1 and 2.

Practice Suggestions

Do these activities together:

1. Point at the notes and say their names. If it is a chord, just say the name of the chord.

2. Point at the notes and say which string they're on, saying "2nd 1st 2nd 1st," etc. If it is a chord, say "strum."

3. Point at the notes and say the finger numbers: "O O O 2." If it is a chord, you can still say the finger numbers—measure 2 would be "1 3 1 rest."

4. Play measures 1 and 2 slowly until comfortable.

5. Play measures 2 and 3 slowly until comfortable.

6. Play measures 1, 2, and 3 slowly until comfortable.

7. Play measures 3 and 4 slowly until comfortable.

8. Play measures 1, 2, 3, and 4 slowly until comfortable.

9. Continue to work through the song in this manner.

Subsequent Lessons

The procedure described in steps 4–9 above is called *additive practice*. This is a great way to quickly master a new piece. Here is a slogan that you and your child should say together, often: SLOW AND STEADY WINS THE RACE.

Notes:

Jumping Around

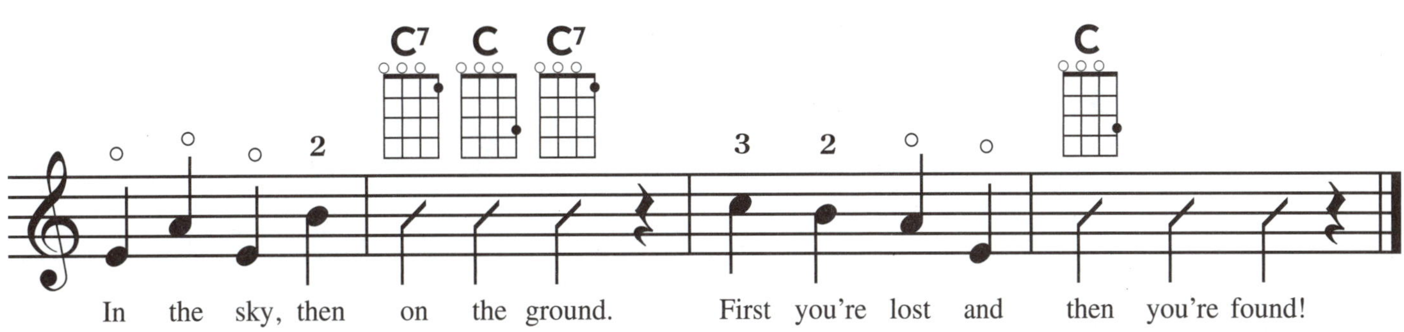

Notes on the Second String: Introducing F

A note on the first space of the staff is called F. Use finger 1 to press the 2nd string at the 1st fret. Pick only the 2nd string. This fingering is the same as for the top fingered note in an F chord.

Introducing the Page

1. Review the F chord (page 27).

2. Draw your child's attention to the picture of the F note on the staff, the fretboard diagram, and the photograph on page 71.

3. Have your child position the left hand as for an F chord, with finger 1 on the 2nd string at the 1st fret, then, instead of strumming, pick just the 2nd string.

4. Congratulate him or her for having learned a new note!

5. Practicing "F Warm-up" will prepare your child for "Ping Pong Song" and "Soccer Game."

6. Notice that in the last measure of "Soccer Game," the 1st finger holds down the F on the 2nd string as you pluck the open 1st string A note. This will require playing on the very tip of the finger, being careful not to interfere with the vibration of the 1st string.

Practice Suggestions

Do these activities together for both songs:

1. Point at the notes and say their names.

2. Point at the notes and say which string they're on.

3. Point at the notes and say the finger numbers.

4. Use additive practice, mastering two measures at a time before adding them to measures previously mastered.

Subsequent Lessons

Practice all songs until secure, confident, and fluent enough to play along with the recording without error or confusion. Ease, accuracy, and confidence will never result from difficulty, error, and insecurity. SLOW AND STEADY WINS THE RACE.

Notes:

A note on the 1st space of the staff is called F. Use finger 1 to press the 2nd string at the 1st fret. Pick only the 2nd string.

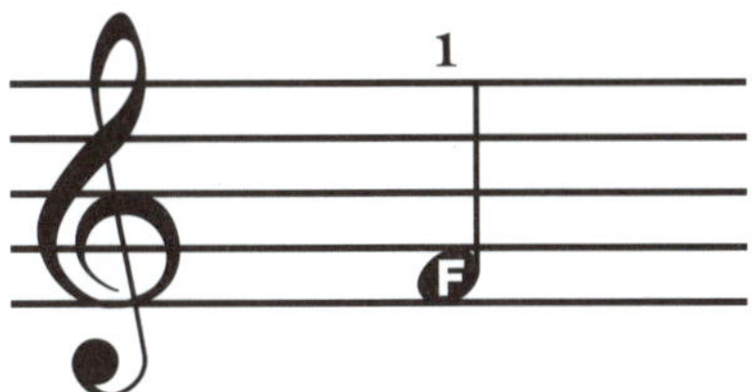

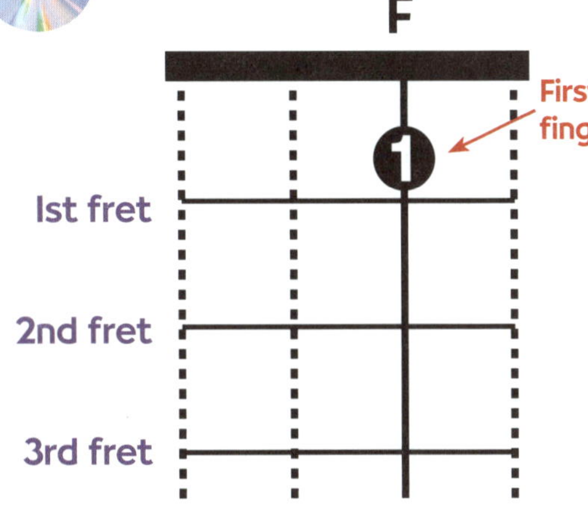

Ping Pong Song

Soccer Game

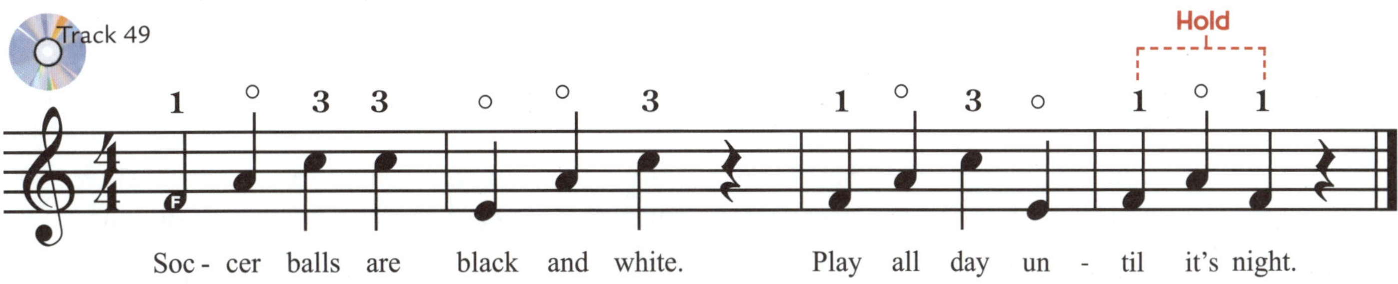

The Half Rest

A *half rest* means do not play for two beats, which is the same as two consecutive quarter rests.

Introducing the Page

1. Draw your child's attention to the half rest on the staff in the yellow box on page 73.

2. Look over "Clap and Count out Loud" with your child and point out the two different kinds of rests used (half rests and quarter rests).

3. Count aloud as you clap the rhythms in the "Clap and Count out Loud" exercise. Spread your hands apart during the rests.

4. Do this together with your child.

When I Feel Best

This song uses lots of the notes your child knows, the G^7 and C chords, and both the quarter and half rests.

Introducing the Page

1. Review the G^7 chord with your child (page 39).

2. Look over the music for "When I Feel Best" together with your child.

3. Notice that finger 1 is used for both the F note and the G^7 chord, so it is most efficient to hold that finger down when switching between the two. Finger 1 is placed on the F note on the third beat of the song and is held down until the last beat of the 5th measure, when it must be lifted to play the E note on the open 2nd string.

Practice Suggestions

Do these activities together with your child:

1. Point at the notes and say their names. Just say the names of the chords.

2. Point at the notes and say which string they're on. Just say "strum" for the chords.

3. Point at the notes and say the finger numbers. For the G7 chord, the fingers are 2–1–3.

4. Use additive practice, mastering two measures at a time before adding them to measures previously mastered.

Subsequent Lessons

Practice "When I Feel Best" for as many days as necessary, until it is smooth, secure, and confident. When your child can play along with Track 51 without error, it is mastered.

The Half Rest

Introducing the Half Rest

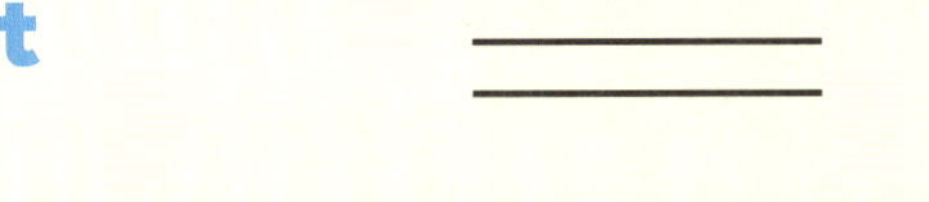

This rest means do not play for two beats, which is the same as ♩ ♩ .

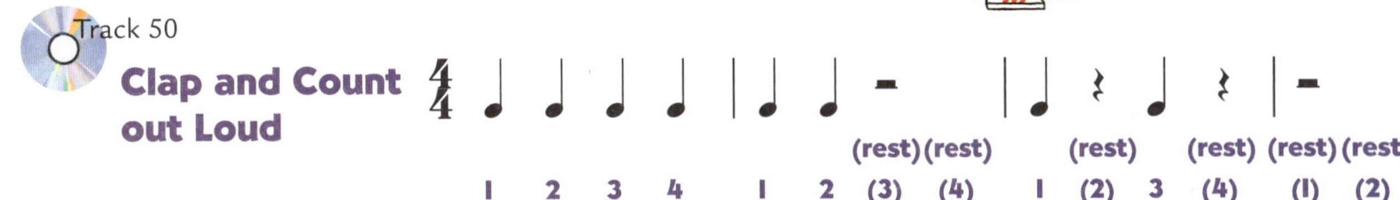

Track 50

Clap and Count out Loud

Practice Tip

Notice that the note F and the G⁷ chord are both fingered with finger 1 at the 1st fret on the 2nd string.

In "When I Feel Best," hold the 1st finger down from the third beat of the 1st measure until the last beat of the 5th measure.

Note F

G⁷ Chord

When I Feel Best

Track 51

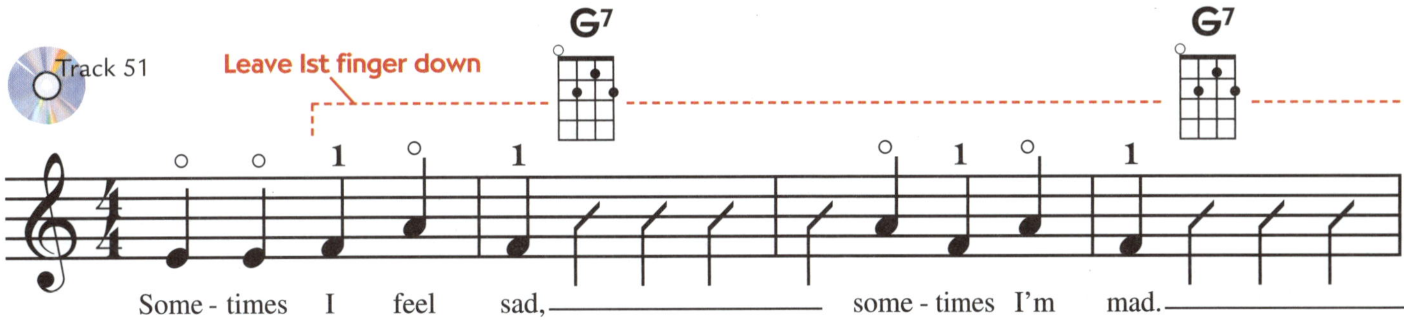

Notes on the Second String: Introducing G

A note on the 2nd line of the staff is called G. The G note is played with the 3rd finger at the 3rd fret of the 2nd string.

Introducing the Page

1. Draw your child's attention to the picture of the G note on the staff, the fretboard diagram, and the photograph on page 75.

2. Practicing "G Warm-up" will prepare your child for "A-Choo!"

3. Count aloud as you clap the rhythms in "A-Choo!" Be sure to spread your hands apart during the rests.

4. Do this together with your child.

5. When possible, it is best to hold down finger 1 while playing finger 3. Make measure 3 an exercise: have your child play it over and over without lifting finger 1. Hold it down while playing the G note with finger 3. If your child's hand is too small or lacks the necessary reach to do this, it's okay. You can try this again after he or she has grown a little.

Practice Suggestions

Do these activities together with your child:

1. Point at the notes and say their names.

2. Point at the notes and say which string they're on.

3. Point at the notes and say the finger numbers.

4. Use additive practice, mastering two measures at a time before adding them to measures previously mastered.

Subsequent Lessons

Practice "A-Choo!" for as many days as necessary, until it is smooth, secure, and confident. When your child can play along with Track 54 without error, it is mastered. If it is possible for them, look for every opportunity to encourage your child to hold finger 1 down while playing finger 3.

Notes:

Notes on the Second String

Introducing G

Hear this note! Track 52

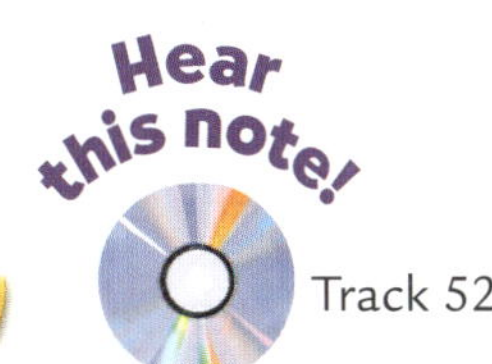

A note on the 2nd line of the staff is called G. Use finger 3 to press the 2nd string at the 3rd fret. Pick only the 2nd string.

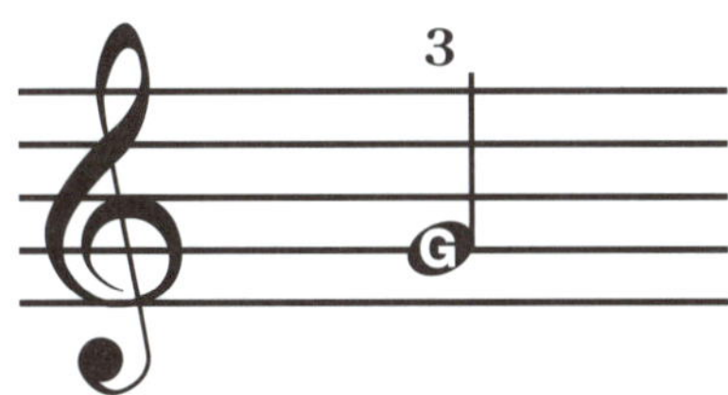

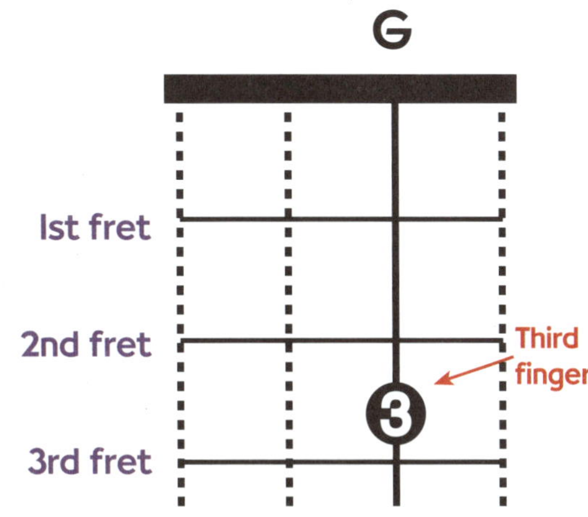

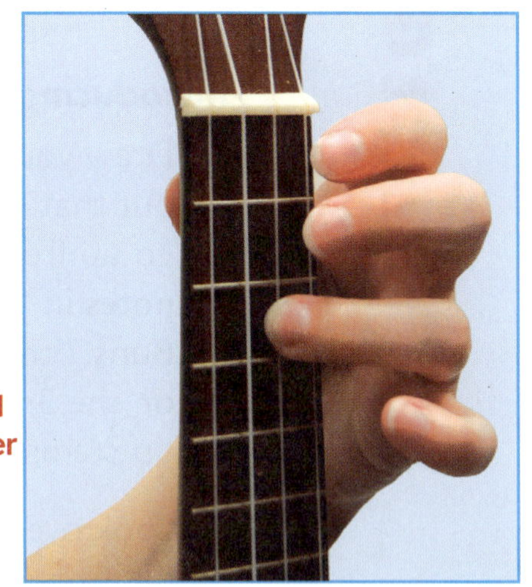

3
G

G
Ist fret
2nd fret
3rd fret
Third finger
3

Track 53

G Warm-up

3
G

A-Choo!

Track 54

○ 1 3 1 3 1 ○
E and F and G are eas - y. Spil - ling pep - per makes me sneez - y.

1 ○ 3 ○ 3 3 3 ○ 3 1 ○ 3 ○
"A - a - choo! A - a - choo!" Pep - per makes me go "A - choo!"

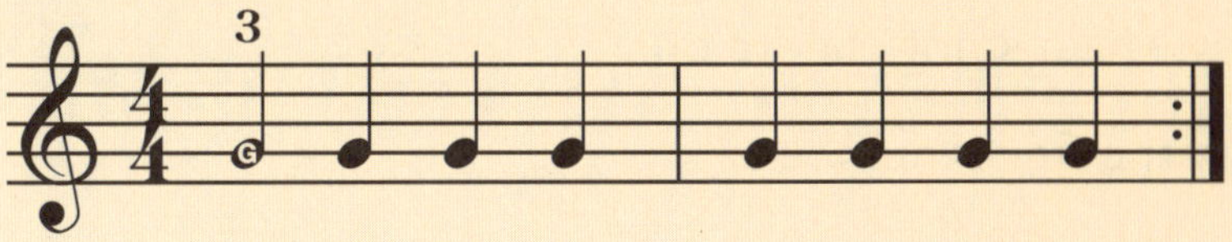

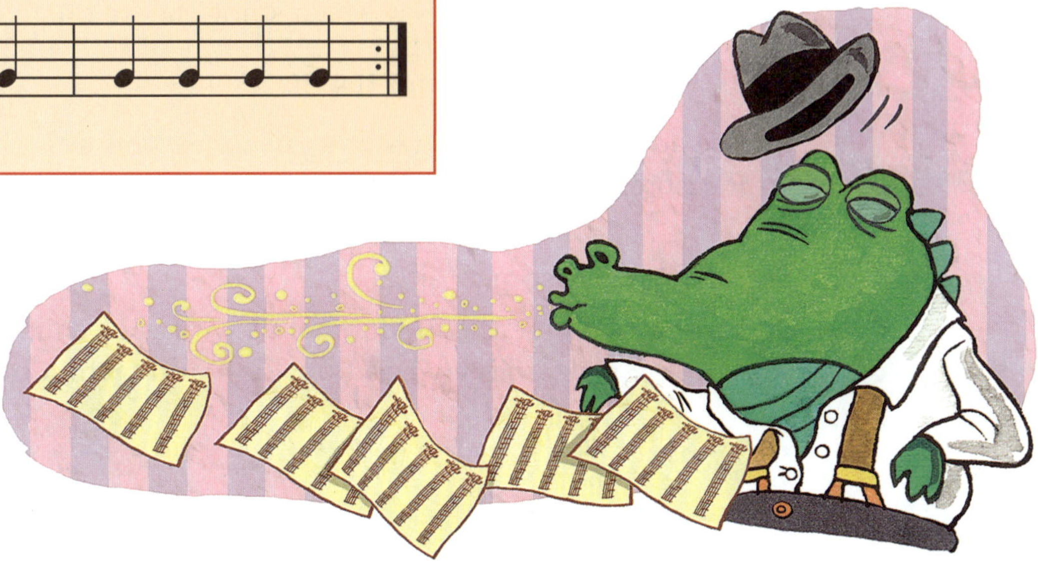

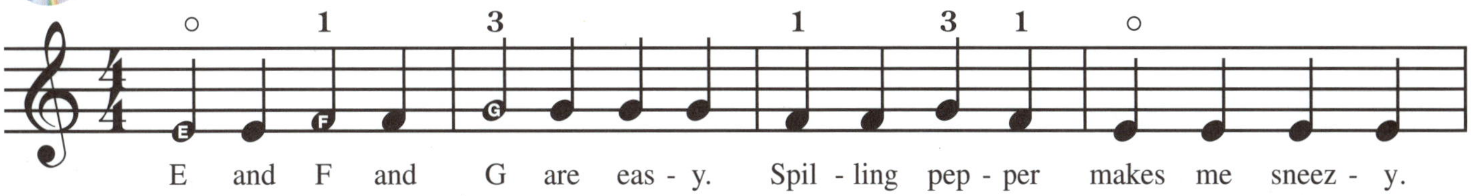

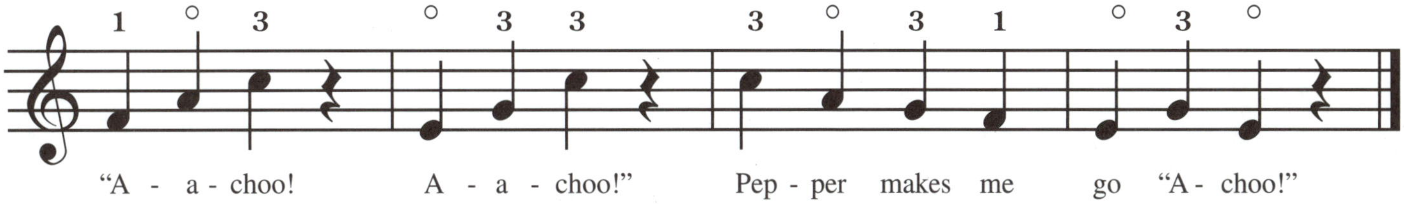

The Half Note

Like the half rest, the *half note* lasts two beats. It is twice as long as a quarter note. By the way, this would be a good time to start singing "Jingle Bells" around the house, even if it is not yet the holiday season. You'll be playing it soon.

Introducing the Page

1. Draw your child's attention to the picture of the half note on page 77. Point out that the note head is an open circle and that it has a stem. The stem can go up from the right side of the note head or down from the left side. The half notes in "Clap and Count out Loud" go up from the right, but in "Hot Cross Buns," they go down from the left as well as up from the right. Generally, notes on the 3rd line or higher have down-stems and notes below that line have up-stems.

2. Look over "Clap and Count out Loud" with your child and point out the two different kinds of notes used (quarter notes and half notes). As you clap, hold your hands together for the two beats of each half note.

Practice Suggestions

Do these activities together with your child:

1. Point at the notes and say their names.

2. Point at the notes and say which string they're on.

3. Point at the notes and say the finger numbers.

4. Use additive practice, mastering two measures at a time before adding them to measures previously mastered.

Subsequent Lessons

Be sure to reinforce the fundamentals with your child: holding the ukulele, how to hold the pick, and left-hand position and technique.

Notes:

The Half Note

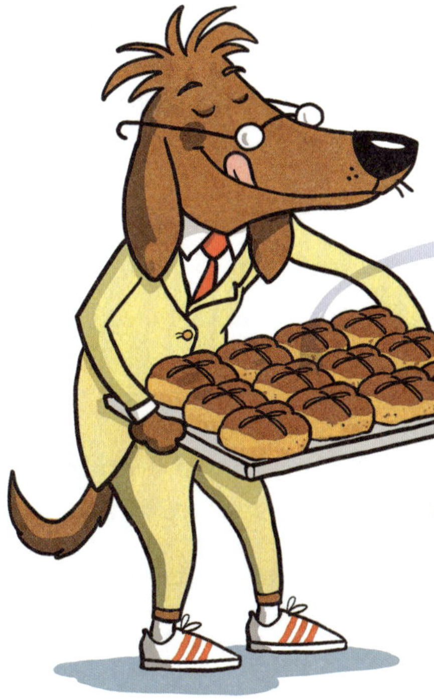

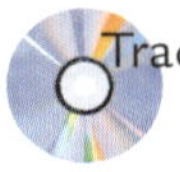

Track 55

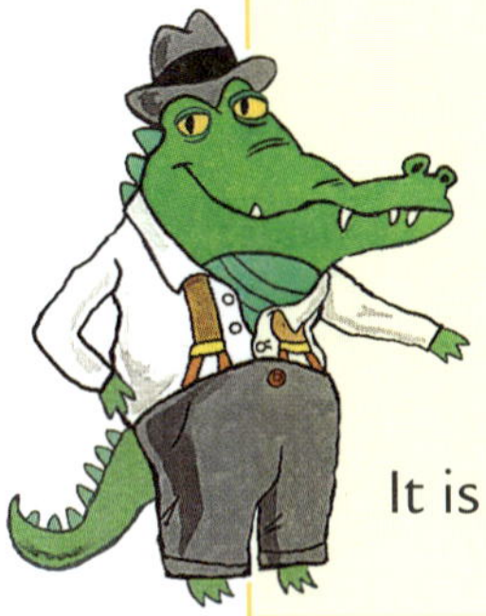

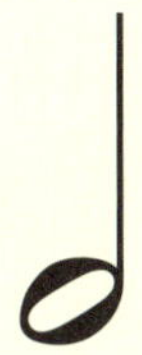

Clap and Count out Loud

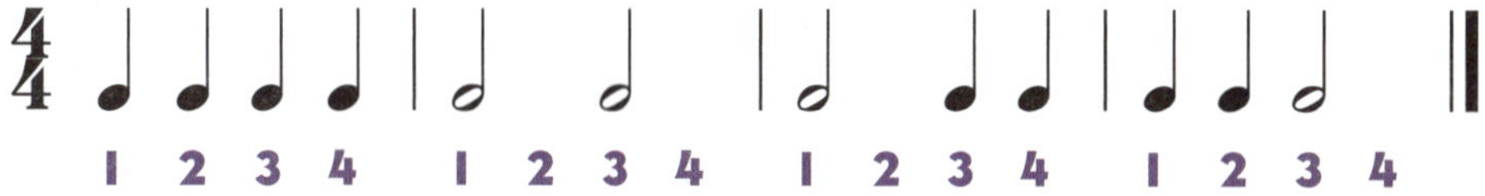

Hot Cross Buns

Track 56

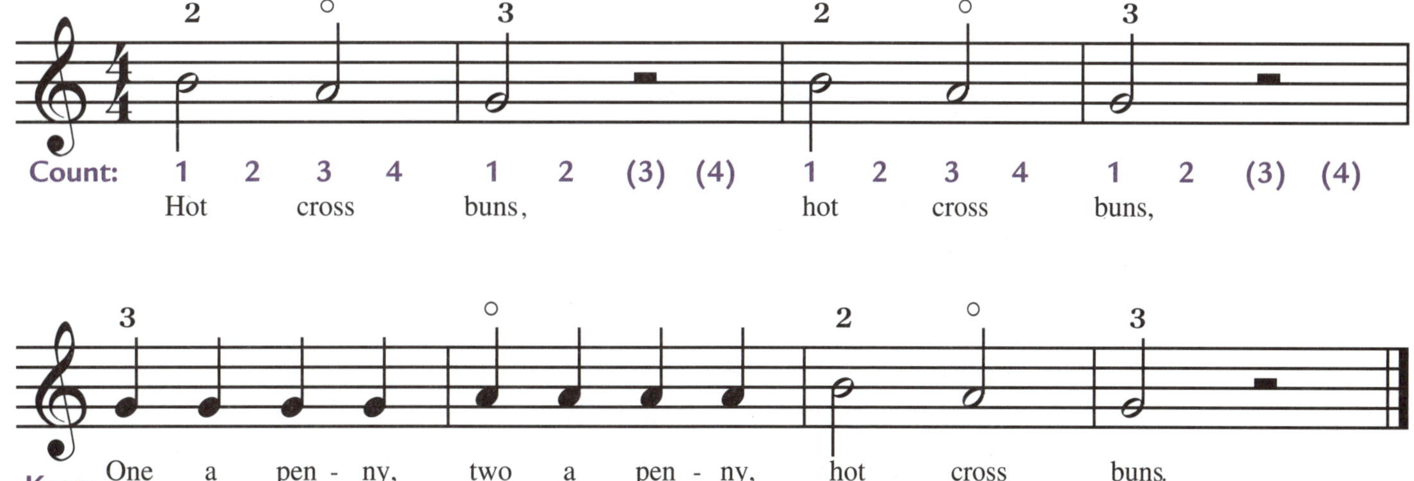

Notes on the Third String: Introducing C

A note on the first *ledger line* below the staff is called C, and it is played by picking the open 3rd string.

Introducing the Page

1. Draw your child's attention to the picture of the C note on the staff and the fretboard diagram on page 79.

2. Practicing "C Warm-up" will prepare your child for "Three Open Strings" and "Little Steps and Big Leaps."

3. Learn "Three Open Strings" first, and make sure your child is comfortable moving the pick (or finger) from string to string.

4. Count aloud as you clap the rhythms in "Little Steps and Big Leaps." Be sure to spread your hands apart during the rests.

5. Do this together with your child.

6. As always, it is best to hold a finger on a note that will be played again very soon. For example, in "Little Steps and Big Leaps," the G note in measure 1, beat 3 is played again in measure 2, beat 1, so it is best to keep finger 3 on or near the 2nd string at the 3rd fret while playing the A note on measure 1, beat 4.

7. The distance from the high C in measure 6 of "Little Steps and Big Leaps" to the low C is called an *octave* (the closest distance between two notes with the same name).

Practice Suggestions

Do these activities together with your child:

1. Point at the notes and say their names.

2. Point at the notes and say which string they're on.

3. Point at the notes and say the finger numbers, saying "O" for open strings.

4. Use additive practice, mastering two measures at a time before adding them to measures previously mastered.

5. Make measure 6 of "Little Steps and Big Leaps" an exercise to repeat many times.

Subsequent Lessons

Practice "Little Steps and Big Leaps" for as many days as necessary, until it is smooth, secure, and confident. When your child can play along with Track 60 without error, it is mastered. Encourage your child to learn to skip from string to string with the pick without looking at the right hand.

Introducing C

Hear this note! — Track 57

A line that extends the staff either up or down is called a *ledger line*. A note one ledger line below the staff is called C. You already know C on the 1st string. This C is the open 3rd string and sounds lower than C on the 1st string. To play this note, pick the open 3rd string.

Three Open Strings

Track 59

Little Steps and Big Leaps

Track 60

The Old Grey Mare

The first thing you'll notice about "The Old Grey Mare" is that it's 17 measures long! It's easy to learn, though, because there is a lot of repetition. This American folk song is about Lady Suffolk, the first race horse recorded as trotting a mile in less than two and a half minutes, in the mid-19th century, when she was 10 years old. That's old for a racehorse!

Introducing the Page

1. The last eight measures start just like measures 2–9. Within those eight measures, measures 8 ad 9 are almost exactly the same as measures 4 and 5. Likewise, measures 12 and 13 are the same as measures 4 and 5.

2. Think of "The Old Grey Mare" as having two sections: The "A" section is measures 1—9, and the "B" section starts on beat 4 of measure 9 and goes till the end. The words of the song (the *lyrics*) make this "A-B" form easy to detect.

3. This song combines a single-note melody with a few strummed chords at the end. Notice, however, that when you strum a chord, the single note just before it is part of the chord. Just leave the finger down, add one more finger, and strum. Easy!

4. Count aloud as you clap the rhythms in "The Old Grey Mare." Be sure to spread your hands apart during the rests.

5. Do this together with your child.

6. Make measures 8 and 9 an exercise to repeat many times; they include lots of string skipping with the pick. See if your child can learn to play these measures without looking at the right hand. It's okay, though, if they need to sneak a peek every now and then. Switching attention from one hand to another and from the hands to the written music is a good skill for your child to develop.

Practice Suggestions

Do these activities together with your child:

1. Point at the notes and say their names.

2. Point at the notes and say which string they're on.

3. Point at the notes and say the finger numbers, saying "O" for open strings. Say "2-O-1-O" for the F chord.

4. Use additive practice, mastering two measures at a time before adding them to measures previously mastered.

Subsequent Lessons

Practice "The Old Grey Mare" for as many days as necessary, until it is smooth, secure, and confident. Sing the song together as your child plays. When your child can play along with Track 61 without error, it is mastered.

The Old Grey Mare

Track 61

Notes on the Third String: Introducing D and the Whole Note

A note in the space directly below the staff is called D. To play a D, use finger 2 to press the 3rd string at the 2nd fret. Pick only the 3rd string. The whole note is an open circle with no stem, and it lasts four beats. Review the G^7 chord on page 39 before starting this page.

Introducing the Page

1. Draw your child's attention to the picture of the D note on the staff, the fretboard diagram, and the photograph on page 83.

2. Practicing "D Warm-up" will prepare your child for "D Is Easy!" and "Taking a Walk."

3. Together, look through "Clap and Count out Loud" and "D Is Easy!," looking for the whole notes. Can your child find them?

4. Practice "Clap and Count out Loud," together.

5. Make measure 3 of "D Is Easy!" an exercise for your child to repeat many times. It includes switching from finger 1 to finger 2 and from the 2nd string to the 3rd string.

6. Master "D Is Easy!" before moving on to "Taking a Walk."

7. Count aloud as you clap the rhythms in "Taking a Walk." Be sure to take your hands apart during the rests.

8. Make measures 5 and 6 of "Taking a Walk" an exercise for your child to repeat. In measure 6, we switch from playing single notes to the G^7 chord. In measure 5, keep finger 2 down on the D and finger 1 down on the F. You'll be more prepared for the G^7 chord in measure 6. Just move finger 3 to the 1st string, 2nd fret, and *voila*! G^7!

Practice Suggestions

Do these activities together with your child:

1. Point at the notes and say their names.

2. Point at the notes and say which string they're on.

3. Point at the notes and say the finger numbers: "2-1-3" for the G7 chord and "O-O-O-3" for the C chord.

4. Use additive practice, mastering two measures at a time before adding them to measures previously mastered.

Subsequent Lessons

Practice "Taking a Walk" for as many days as necessary, until it is smooth, secure, and confident. When your child can play along with Track 66 without error and without looking at the right hand, it is mastered.

Introducing D

A note on the space below the staff is called D. Use finger 2 to press the 3rd string at the 2nd fret. Pick only the 3rd string.

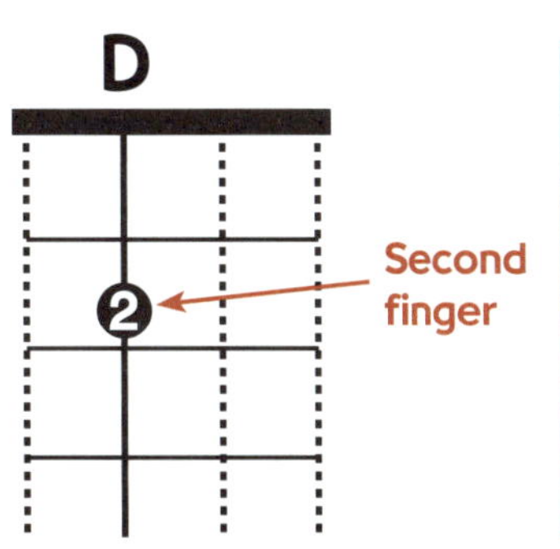

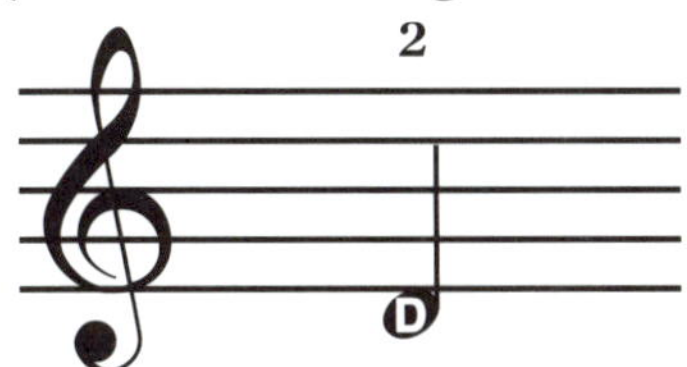

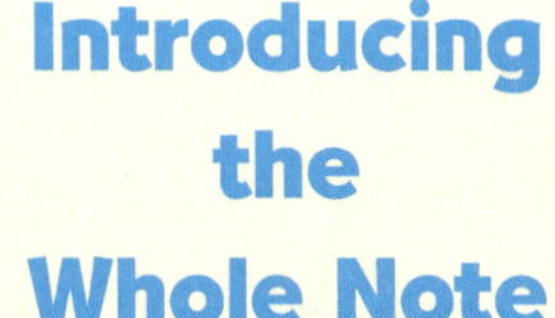
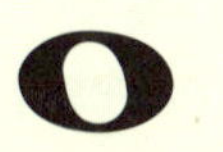

Clap and Count out Loud

D Is Easy!

Taking a Walk

Ode to Joy

"Ode to Joy" is a theme from the fourth movement of Beethoven's monumental *9th Symphony*. Written for a symphony orchestra and a large chorus, it remains one of the most popular classical works. More importantly, it's fun and easy to play on a ukulele!

Introducing the Page

1. The first four measures are almost exactly repeated in the last four measures except for the very last measure.

2. The whole melody is played on the 2nd and 3rd strings.

Practice Suggestions

Do these activities together with your child:

1. Point at the notes and say their names.

2. Point at the notes and say which string they're on.

3. Point at the notes and say the finger numbers.

4. Use additive practice, mastering two measures at a time before adding them to measures previously mastered.

Subsequent Lessons

Be sure to reinforce the fundamentals with your child: holding the ukulele, how to hold the pick, and left-hand position and technique. Also, find a recording of Beethoven's *9th Symphony* and listen to it around the house. When the 4th Movement is playing, does your child recognize the "Ode to Joy" melody? Singing and listening to music are both part of learning to play. Keep your child engaged in music in as many ways as you can. It will provide entertainment for the whole family.

Notes:

Ode to Joy
from Beethoven's 9th Symphony

Track 67

Jingle Bells

"Jingle Bells" features the C and G^7 chords, quarter rests, and notes on both the 1st and 2nd strings. This would be a good time to start singing "Mary Had a Little Lamb" around the house. It's the next song in this book.

Introducing the Page

1. Review the music with your child, pointing out the half notes, chord strums, and quarter rests. Quarter notes comprise the rest of the song.

2. Make the last two measures an exercise for your child to repeat. It combines the biggest challenges in this song: reaching from finger 3 to finger 1, switching from single notes to chord strums, and using the rest position to perform the quarter rest.

Practice Suggestions

Do these activities together with your child:

1. Point at the notes and say their names. Just say the names of the chords.

2. Point at the notes and say which string they're on.

3. Point at the notes and say the finger numbers.

4. Use additive practice, mastering two measures at a time before adding them to measures previously mastered.

5. Sing while you play. It's fun!

Subsequent Lessons

1. Review "Jingle Bells" as needed.

2. Play "Jingle Bells" with Track 68 of the recording.

Notes:

Jingle Bells

Mary Had a Little Lamb

"Mary Had a Little Lamb" has all of the same notes, chords, and rests as "Jingle Bells." It is another chance to enjoy playing music with the skills and knowledge your child has learned so far. This is a good time to start singing "Over the Rainbow" around the house. It's coming up soon!

Introducing the Page

1. Review the music with your child, pointing out the half notes, chord strums, and quarter rests. As with "Jingle Bells," quarter notes comprise the rest of the song.

2. Make measure 4 an exercise for your child to repeat. It's a great exercise for learning to prepare a chord fingering while playing single notes. While playing the G note on the 2nd string at the 3rd fret, you can prepare fingers 1 and 2 on their respective frets for the G^7 chord. Finger 1 will go on the 2nd string at the 1st fret, and finger 2 will go on the 3rd string and the 2nd fret. Then, on beat 4 of the measure, move finger 3 to the 1st string at the 2nd fret; it should be a very small, direct finger movement with a slight leftward rotation at the wrist.

3. In measure 8, just pluck the C note on the open 3rd string and then strum all four strings to play the C chord.

4. Line 3 is the same as line 1, and line 4 is the same as line 2.

Practice Suggestions

Do these activities together with your child:

1. Point at the notes and say their names. Just say the names of the chords.

2. Point at the notes and say which string they're on.

3. Point at the notes and say the finger numbers.

4. Use additive practice, mastering two measures at a time before adding them to measures previously mastered.

5. Sing while you play!

Subsequent Lessons

1. Review "Mary Had a Little Lamb" as needed.

2. Play "Mary Had a Little Lamb" with Track 69 of the recording.

Notes:

Mary Had a Little Lamb

Over the Rainbow

Ever since the Hawaiian ukulelist Israel "Iz" Ka'ano'i Kamakawiwo'ole (better known as just "Iz") had a platinum hit with his interpretation of this much-loved song from the movie *The Wizard of Oz*, it has been a favorite among ukulele enthusiasts. You and your child have accomplished a *lot* to have arrived here, at this beloved ukulele song! Congratulations!

Introducing the Page

1. Review the music with your child, pointing out the half notes, chord strums, and quarter rests.

2. Measures 1 and 2, and 5 and 6 will make great exercises for practicing switching from plucking single notes to strumming chords. Master both of these two-measure exercises and it will be easy to learn to play the whole song.

3. In measure 1, you can prepare the 3rd finger on the 1st string at the 3rd fret for the C chord while the open low C note is ringing, and then keep it there for the single note high C and chord strums in measure 2.

4. In measure 9, you can prepare the fingers on the F chord while the open A note is ringing, then keep the fingers down through the end of measure 10.

Practice Suggestions

Do these activities together with your child:

1. Point at the notes and say their names. Just say the names of the chords.

2. Point at the notes and say which string they're on.

3. Point at the notes and say the finger numbers.

4. Use additive practice, mastering two measures at a time before adding them to measures previously mastered.

5. Sing while you play!

Subsequent Lessons

1. Review "Over the Rainbow" as needed.

2. Play "Over the Rainbow" with Track 70 of the recording.

3. Find a recording of Iz playing and singing this song! It will be a pleasure the whole family can enjoy together.

Notes:

Over the Rainbow

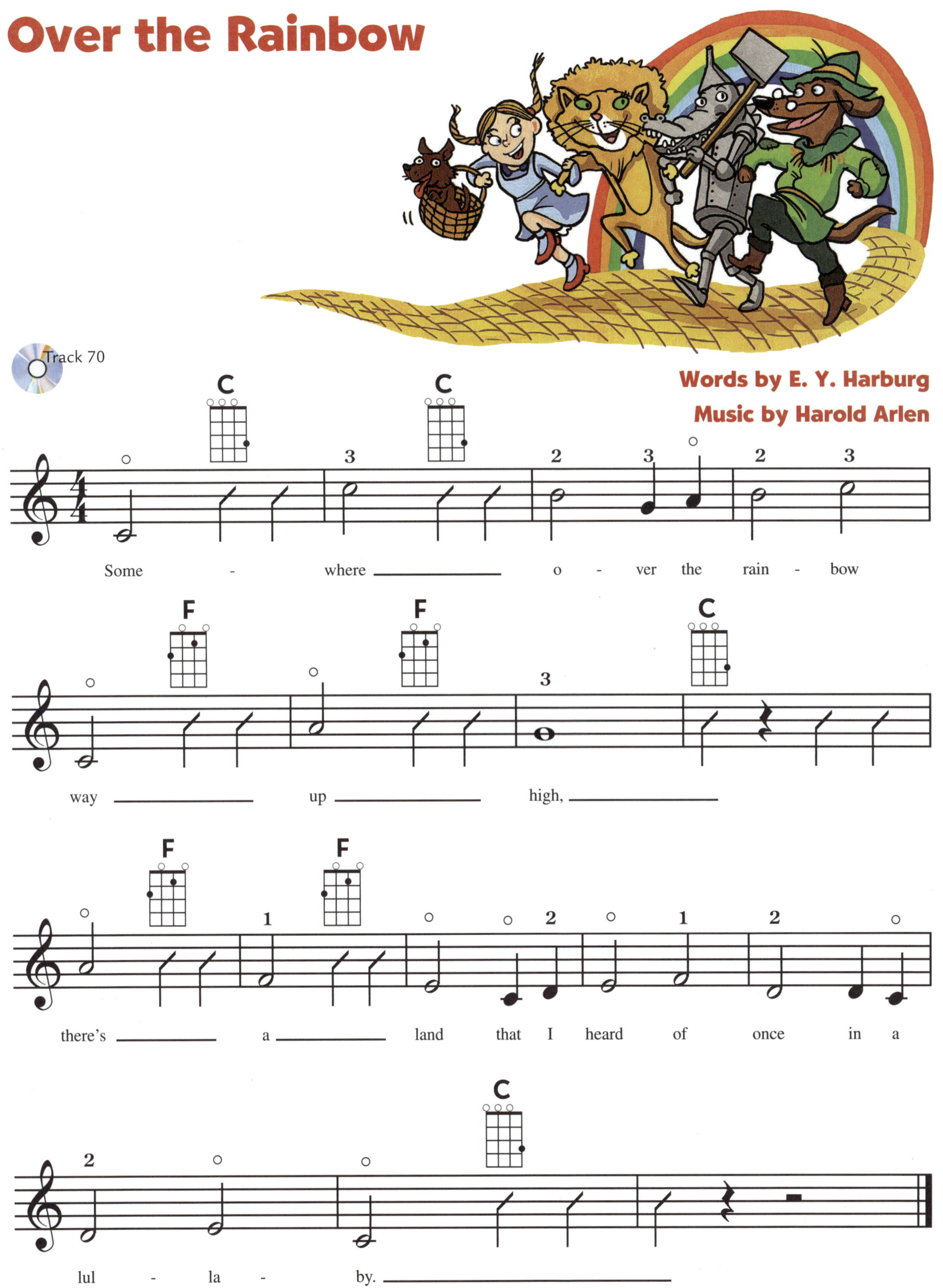

Music Matching Games

Completing the fun matching games
on page 93 will be a great review for
your child. Enjoy!

Notes:

Music Matching Games

Chords

Draw a line to match each chord frame on the left to the correct photo on the right.

1. 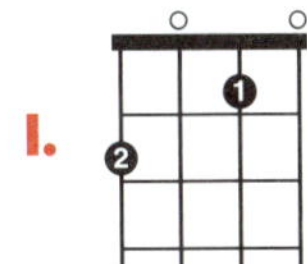   

2.    

3.    

4. 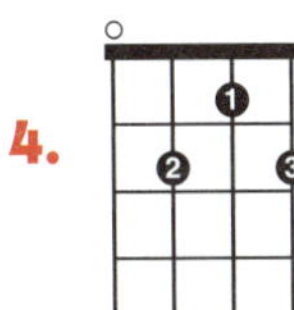   

Symbols

Draw a line to match each symbol on the left to its name on the right.

1.   Treble clef

2.   Quarter note

3.   Whole note

4.   Quarter slash

5.   Half note

6.   Double bar line

7.   Half rest

8.   Repeat sign

9.    Quarter rest

Notes

Draw a line to match each note on the left to its correct music notation on the right.

1.    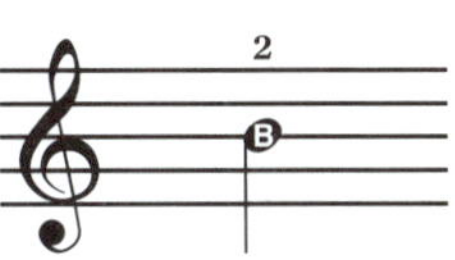

2.    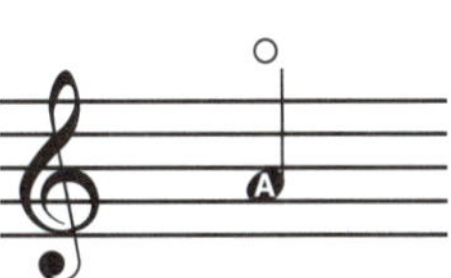

3.    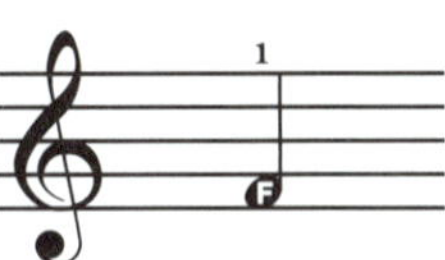

4.    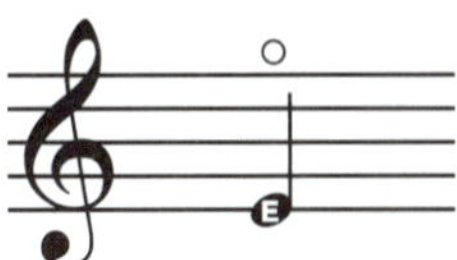

5.    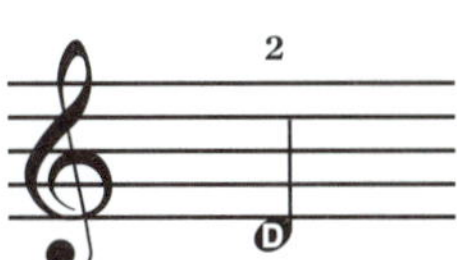

6. 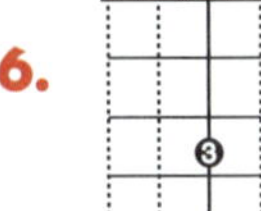   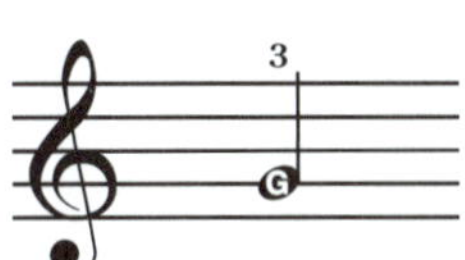

7. 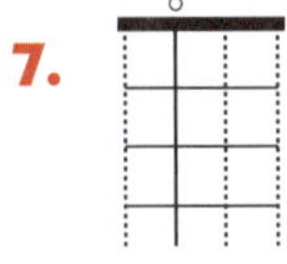   

8. 

Answer Key

Chords
1: page 27; 2: page 23; 3: page 19; 4: page 39

Symbols
1: page 83; 2: page 77; 3: page 53; 4: page 15;
5: page 51; 6: page 35; 7: page 73; 8: page 21;
9: page 15

Notes
1: page 55; 2: page 59; 3: page 63; 4: page 67;
5: page 71; 6: page 75; 7: page 79; 8: page 83

Certificate of Completion

Complete the certificate on the next page and congratulate your child. This is an important achievement, so make sure to celebrate with a treat! Put this certificate on the wall above your lesson area or in a prominent place.

Notes:

Certificate of Promotion
This certifies that
has mastered and perfected
Alfred's Teach Your Child To Play Ukulele, Book 1
Teacher / Parent
Date

Frequently Asked Questions

How long should the lesson last and how frequently should they occur?

Lessons should be held once or twice weekly and should last 30 to 45 minutes depending on the age and attention span of your child. Another possibility would be to spend a few minutes together every day. While lesson time should be special time—devoted specifically to a ukulele lesson—don't try to structure time too strictly. Your child may have questions and want to chat about the lesson content. The lesson should be engaging and fun.

How much material should be covered in each lesson?

The amount of material covered in your lesson time will vary. You can gauge this by how well your child plays the current piece, how long it takes to review the previous lesson's material, and the complexity of the new material.

How long should a student continue with each piece?

A piece is mastered when it can be played at an appropriate *tempo* (speed) without error. An excellent way to judge the proficiency with which your child plays a given piece or song is for them to play along with the recording. If your child cannot play along with the audio without stopping, or without error or difficulty, they probably need more time with the piece.

Each piece should present a reasonable challenge to the student. If they master the material immediately, you should be presenting more challenging lessons. If a piece takes weeks and weeks to master, it is too difficult and you should try presenting less challenging material. If a skill, concept, or piece does not improve with practice, make sure your child is practicing slowly and carefully, using additive practice (page 68) and mastering just a few measures at a time, building up speed bit by bit. Remember, ease, accuracy, and confidence will never arise from difficulty, error, or confusion.

What should I do when my child finishes this book?

Move on to Alfred's *Teach Your Child to Play Ukulele 2* (43997) and apply the principles you learned in this book to continue teaching your child to play.